A WOMAN IN THE POLAR NIGHT

'If I only read one book each winter it would be this small slim volume. It's an extraordinary true fable that sings the songs of the old Arctic and leaves your heart ringing with cold, wild delight'
GEOGRAPHICAL

'Extraordinary… a radical, feminist text that speaks to the disconnection from the rest of nature we are experiencing at unprecedented levels today. It's hard to believe it was written over 80 years ago'
INDEPENDENT

A
WOMAN
IN THE
POLAR NIGHT

CHRISTIANE RITTER

TRANSLATED FROM THE GERMAN
BY JANE DEGRAS

WITH A FOREWORD
BY SARA WHEELER

PUSHKIN PRESS CLASSICS

Pushkin Press
Somerset House, Strand
London WC2R 1LA

Original text © 2010 Ullstein Buchverlage GmbH, Berlin
English translation © Jane Degras 1954
Foreword © Sara Wheeler 2019

A Woman in the Polar Night was first published as *Eine Frau erlebt die Polarnacht* in 1938

First published in English in 1954 by George Allen & Unwin Ltd, London

First published by Pushkin Press in 2019
This edition published 2024

9 8 7 6 5 4 3 2 1

ISBN 13: 978-1-80533-089-9

All interior photographs courtesy of Bjørn Klauer at Huskyfarm huskyfarm.de
Photographs printed with permission of Karin Ritter
Map hand-drawn by Neil Gower
Designed and typeset by Tetragon, London
Printed and bound in the United Kingdom by Clays Ltd, Elcograf S.p.A.

www.pushkinpress.com

Contents

Sven Ohlson's Hut

Biscay Hook

Verlegen Hook

Welcome Point

Mossel Bay

The Hut at Grey Hook

Magdalena Bay

Sydgatt

REINDEERLAND

Liefde Bay

Cape Roos

Bock Bay

Svendsen Bay

Wood Bay

Bangen Hook

N E W

Cross Point

West Fjord

Cape Petermann

W I L D E B A Y

Kings Bay

W E S T

Holtedahl Plateau

S P I T S B E R G E N

Dickson Bay

G R E E N L A N D

S E A

Ice Fjord

Sassen Bay

Advent Anchorage

LONGYEAR VALLEY

NORTH EAST LAND

N.G.

Sorge Bay

Hinlopen Strait

FRIESLAND

BARENTS SEA

BARENTS ISLAND

N

Hilmar Nois' Cabin

0   km   30

0   miles   30

Foreword

In these pages, first published in 1938, Christiane Ritter conjures the rasp of the ski runner, the scent of burning blubber and the rippling iridescence of the Northern Lights. Her prose is as pared as Arctic ice. As her adopted country languishes "in bluish grey shadow", the author discovers, with childlike delight, the uncluttered nature of life in the Norwegian Arctic, where "everything is concerned with simple being".

Ritter's husband Hermann had taken part in a scientific expedition in Spitsbergen and stayed on, fishing from his cutter in summer and in winter, when everything was frozen, hunting for furs. The Austrian Ritter, who was in her mid-thirties (she was born in 1897), did not follow at once, but when Hermann asked her to join him as "housewife" for a winter, she accepted. Before leaving home in 1933, she said that to her "the Arctic was just another word for freezing and forsaken solitude".

The reader does not know why Hermann had chosen to be absent from the family home for so long. The couple had a teenage daughter who is not mentioned in the book.

They live in a small hut at Grey Hook on the north coast of Spitsbergen; an amiable Norwegian hunter called Karl

Nicholaisen joins them there. Their nearest neighbour, an old Swede, is in another hut sixty miles away (so "it won't be too lonely for you", Hermann wrote to his wife apparently without irony). The trio have supplies, but the two men must hunt if they are to survive.

Svalbard, Ritter explains, "is the old Norwegian name for Spitsbergen", and it means "Cold Coast". In fact, the archipelago, of which Ritter's island was the largest, had been renamed Svalbard a few years before the author's occupancy. Spitsbergen remains the official name of that one island, one of the world's northernmost inhabited places. Though it was barely inhabited in the author's day: early peoples never got that far after trekking east across the strait now called Bering and beyond.

First impressions are bleak.

> The scene is comfortless. Far and wide not a tree or shrub; everything grey and bare and stony. The boundlessly broad foreland, a sea of stone, stones stretching up to the crumbling mountains and down to the crumbling shore, an arid picture of death and decay.

"A beast of a stove" leaves the hut coated in soot at all times, a state of affairs Hermann, fastidious in lower latitudes, calmly accepts. "How Spitsbergen has changed him," notes Ritter. She acknowledges "horror and dread", though doesn't tell her husband how she feels. When she arrives her eyes smart from unending daylight; then comes the long night, with its psychological challenges. She experiences *rar*, the Norwegian word for the strangeness that afflicts many who overwinter in the polar regions. All indigenous languages, such as Inuktitut, have a word for *rar*. Norwegian hunters apparently used to say *ishavet kaller*, or "the Arctic calls", when one of their comrades hurled himself into the sea for no reason. But the author's moments of despair are just that—momentary. Then she begins, maniacally, to sew, mend and polish.

Ritter has her own room in the hut (it is six feet by four, with an inch of ice on the walls), and sometimes moonlight filters green through the small snowed-up window. For a month the trio have a light cycle, during which they collect birch bark born on the tide for kindling, then darkness takes over: that chapter is called "The Earth Sinks into Shadow". Arctic foxes change colour, ptarmigans lose their spots, and everything freezes. I was in the polar regions once during the onset of winter. Night rolls in like a tide: it is one of the greatest seasonal events on the planet, akin to the rising of sap. (The author uses the adjective "titanic" three times to describe it.) In the smoky hut the trio play cards, though the wretched stove has rendered the hearts and diamonds as black as the spades and clubs. And of course they tell one another stories—often the same ones many times over.

Anxieties over the availability of fresh meat run through the book like a Greek chorus, and Karl and Hermann set out again and again to find seal, bear, ptarmigan and duck. "It is grotesque how carefree they are", the author writes early on, acutely aware of the perils of the situation, though she eventually gets into the rhythm of life, and begins to cherish the beauty and simplicity of the far north. This emotional transformation gives the book a shape beyond the practicalities of the story.

She goes hunting with the men both before and after the light vanishes, sometimes on a Nansen sledge with the temperature hovering at a sprightly minus 38 degrees Celsius. Out in their small motorboat one time, "we are seized by an over-brimming sense of happiness in our worldwide freedom, in the complete absence of any restraint". At the same time Ritter appreciates the men's prowess: "The lives of these hunters," she writes, "are a series of performances that are almost inhuman."

Astonishingly, she spends many days and nights alone in the sooty hut when the others are hunting, on one occasion during a nine-day storm. "If a bear comes near the hut," the men say as they leave, "shoot him. It's best to hit him in the breast, and even if he looks as though he is dead, shoot him again in the head." And this to a young woman who had grown up with cooks and servants and drivers.

She tackles seal-blood pancakes, sews the long seams of the fur sleeping bags and listens to the frozen corpses of skinned foxes knocking on the roof where they have been tied down. She learns icecraft, even when she has to crawl on all fours outdoors on account of the murderous wind. The emotional climax of the book arrives when she is alone in this storm, battling the stove, battling everything.

I stayed in a hunter's hut in Svalbard once. I didn't have to shoot my own dinner though, and I had high-tech kit and a radio. I could have left at any time; when a ship dropped Ritter off, the captain said he would be back in a year to pick her up. Karl admitted later that he had thought Ritter wouldn't cope, but after it was over he told another explorer that she was "one hell of a woman".

They make Christmas gifts, including a pair of salad servers carved out of a mahogany table leg washed ashore, and celebrate New Year's Eve with raspberry juice and surgical spirit. Cheers!

Just living takes a long time in the Arctic. Ritter skies down to a freshwater spring to rinse the laundry, a ski stick in one hand and a bucket of clothes in the other. "It is a slow job," she notes nonchalantly, "to get along in the dark." Small pleasures are attenuated in the polar regions. "To celebrate the return of the sunshine we have a whole spoonful of honey with our coffee and cold seal." And as all polar hands note, a paucity of reading material renders old newspapers gripping. She quotes a "fascinating" advertising section, which includes, "Coffins, good, solid, cheap. Shrouds and wreaths also supplied. Hans Dahl, Storgt. 106."

She has a gift for the telling phrase: a slaughtered seal is slit up and "laid open like a book". (Should she bake the flippers, she wonders?) Ritter leavens the prose with yeasty direct speech, and the book is fluently translated by Jane Degras. The author went on to enjoy a career as a painter, and she has a visual imagination and an eye for colour. As twilight falls she writes of

> scenes that remind us so strongly of the delicate, wonderful paintings of the Chinese painter-monks, in which the immense and mysterious effect is achieved entirely by gradations from light to dark grey, by forms indicated rather than outlines.

The sky lightens to "a tender cobalt" at the horizon, a "pale yellow brightness" spreads from the east, and the frozen sea "shines like an immense opal". And of course, there are the Northern Lights:

their bright rays, shooting downward, look like gleaming rods
of glass. They break out from a tremendous height and seem
to be falling directly toward me, growing brighter and clearer,
in radiant lilacs, greens, and pinks, swinging and whirling
around their own axis in a wild dance.

Heavenly music indeed. Rare flashes of sentiment add dashes
of another kind of colour. When she tries to take a photograph, Ritter says, "It seems to me a deadly sin to steal a piece
of this supernatural scene and carry it away with me." (As
it turned out the camera jammed and froze, so no sinning
was involved.) In a moment of spiritual awakening she says,
"I divine the ultimate salvation before which all human reasoning dissolves into nothing." But the author is too much
of a natural writer to put much of this in: the book is mostly
about ice and soot.

She comes to experience deep pleasure, and is immensely
moved by the landscape, linking its shifts to human mutability.
"Why has so little been written about the great transition stage
in Arctic nature?" she wonders.

It is precisely at this time that a decisive change takes place in
the human mood, when the reality of the phenomenal world
dissolves, when men slowly lose all sense of fixed points, of
impulses from the external world.

Ritter died in 2000 at the age of 103, never having written
anything else. *A Woman in the Polar Night* was a bestseller
throughout Europe and has never been out of print in German.
It remains among my all-time favourite polar books, mixing

the lightest touch of reflection with solid facts about how the trio ever survived. Ritter made me believe that the Big White really did change her—without any of the pyrotechnics of contemporary "transformation" memoirs, of which there are too many. Before Ritter's departure Helmer Hansen had given her advice on gear ("get felt socks"): he had been to the South Pole with Amundsen. A pleasing example of historical context. *A Woman in the Polar Night* is a period piece.

As for the end of the volume—well, you'll see what happens at the end when you get there. Women's voices are seldom heard in the polar regions. Unlike most male accounts, this one is not about breaking records or beating the Arctic into submission like a mammoth outside a cave. A short while after Ritter's return from the far north her husband's family estate burned to the ground. But she had learned equanimity in Svalbard. "A year in the Arctic should be compulsory to everyone," she would say regularly later in life. "Then you will come to realise what's important in life and what isn't."

In these pages what Christiane Ritter calls "holy quiet" descends on the reader like a benediction.

—SARA WHEELER, 2019

A WOMAN
IN THE
POLAR NIGHT

I

The Beckoning Arctic

To live in a hut in the Arctic had always been my husband's wish-dream. Whenever anything went wrong in our European home, a short circuit, a burst pipe, or even if the rent was raised, he would always say that nothing like that could happen in a hut in the Arctic.

After taking part in a scientific expedition, my husband remained in Spitsbergen, fishing in the Arctic from his cutter, and in winter, when everything was frozen over, hunting for furs on the mainland. Letters and telegrams used to come from the far north: "Leave everything as it is and follow me to the Arctic."

But for me at that time, as for all central Europeans, the Arctic was just another word for freezing and forsaken solitude. I did not follow at once.

Then gradually the diaries that arrived in summer from the far north began to fascinate me. They told of journeys by water and over ice, of the animals and the fascination of the wilderness, of the strange light over the landscape, of the strange illumination of one's own self in the remoteness of the polar night. In his descriptions there was practically never any mention of cold or darkness, of storms or hardships.

The little winter hut appeared to me in a more and more friendly light. As housewife I would not have to accompany him on the dangerous winter excursions. I could stay by the warm stove in the hut, knit socks, paint from the window, read thick books in the remote quiet and, not least, sleep to my heart's content.

The decision to hazard a winter's stay ripened in my mind. I made careful preparations, for I wanted to set foot in the Arctic well protected, as though I were sitting in a warm comfortable seat in the cinema, with all the events and the unfamiliar beauty of the polar night unrolling before me. Mothers, grandmothers, and aunts knitted warm wraps; fathers, uncles, and brothers presented me with the latest heating equipment. Just the same, they kept telling me that it was hare-brained idiocy for a woman to go to the Arctic.

The latest letter arrived from my husband:

I hope you're going to keep your promise and come up here this year. I've taken over for next winter a little hut on the north coast of Spitsbergen. It's supposed to be well and strongly built. It won't be too lonely for you because at the northeast corner of the coast, about sixty miles from here, there is another hunter living, an old Swede. We can visit him in the spring when it's light again and the sea and fjords are frozen over.

Apart from your ski boots, you don't need to bring anything. There are skis and equipment here left over from a previous travelling companion. I'll see about provisions and everything else needed for the winter.

Don't bring anything more than you can yourself comfortably carry in a rucksack. There's a very good opportunity for us to make the journey. We shall row straight across the Ice Fjord from Advent Anchorage with the hunter Nois. Then he will take us on in his dog sleigh over the glacier, and from there we'll go on alone, across the Wijde Fjord straight on. At the most we'll have to cross a few glacier streams. We can get to our house on the north coast in about fourteen days.

Telegraph me at once what ship you'll be coming on. I will radio-telegraph you later onboard ship instructions about where to disembark.

P.S. If you still have room in your rucksack, bring enough toothpaste for two people for a year, and also sewing needles.

A few hours after receiving this letter I had bought my sailing ticket and telegraphed my husband the name of the ship and the date of its sailing. Only then did I give way to the disgust I felt because I was to take no luggage with me. The things I had got ready! Apart from equipment, a feather bed, and hot-water bottles, there were books to read and books to write in, paint boxes and films, baking powder and spices, wool for knitting and wool for darning. What wouldn't be needed for a whole year in the Arctic wilderness, with a man who for all I knew had himself grown wild in the last few years…

And why, of all places, must he choose the north coast to winter on? Why choose a coast that, as far as I knew, was besieged by drift ice practically the whole year round, difficult for ships to get at, and two hundred and fifty miles away from the nearest human settlement, the other side of the glaciers and fjords?

Despondently I packed the most essential things into a rucksack. The rest—piles of it—I packed into old trunks and sea chests and took them with me. They would have to be left on a lonely Spitsbergen shore unless a happy accident brought my goods and chattels to their destination.

It was a burning hot day in July when, dressed in my ski outfit, wearing hobnailed boots and carrying on my back a towering rucksack, I waited at our little station, surrounded by relatives who had come to bid me farewell, as well as the cook, the gardener, and the laundry woman. They were still shaking their heads in disapproval, but at the same time pressing on me little packages, things that were, they said, "indispensable" for the Arctic; I must take them with me and not look at them until I got on board.

"If the stove doesn't work properly, come back on the last autumn ship," my mother called out anxiously as the train drew out.

2

Outward Bound

Rather indifferently, I watch the bustle as our ship starts to move out of the harbour at Hamburg. Before my inner eye the broad calm of the far north rises already, but around me a thousand people are waving and blowing their noses as the ship's orchestra plays a sentimental farewell song. The passengers are hiring deck chairs, invading the coffee lounge, storming the currency exchange booth—people from the big city, with the haste of the big city, at the beginning of a four-weeks polar cruise.

I flee to my cabin and inspect the gifts from my family. I am touched. The Bible, printed on thin paper, from Papa; some camel-hair clothes from Mama; an unbreakable mirror from my sisters; dried parsley from the gardener; kitchen spoons and a whisk from the cook, and from the laundry woman a medieval Tobias amulet to keep me safe against all evil spirits.

The passengers who share my cabin come in and look with disapproval at my suspicious-looking luggage. But to avoid notice, as I do not want my plans for the winter to get around the ship, I cannot solve the puzzle for them.

The next day the hubbub onboard ship dies down. The fourteen hundred restless passengers lie sleeping on their fourteen hundred deck chairs, with a relaxed holiday air, and I go to find out if my big luggage has been put safely onboard. From a corner of the large, empty, dimly lit baggage room a rather clumsy figure rises.

"Oho, little miss, so you're the lady who wants to go to Spitsbergen?"

"But how do you know?"

"But it's written on your luggage. Tell me, why do you want to go to that godforsaken island?" The fat old baggage master looks at me sympathetically over his spectacles as he fills out a freight sheet.

"No special reason… to see the polar lights."

"For the university?"

"No, just for me."

"Well, you c'n get that outer your head. You'll freeze to death on that there island. You won't fit in there at all. An' you c'n get scurvy there too. They say that if you sleep well twice runnin', it's a sign you'll get the scurvy. I c'n tell you a thing or two. I used to be in the health service."

"Thank you, I'd rather you didn't. But you will be kind enough to see that my luggage is taken off, won't you?"

"Where are you going to land in Spitsbergen?"

"I wish I knew. I haven't the least idea."

"You see. Why don't you come back home all nice with us? Our captain won't let you off the ship. You don't know him. He won't allow anything like that!"

This frightens me a little. "Where can I find the captain?" I ask the baggage master.

"Up there." With his index finger he points straight up, as though to the sky. "Up there, on the captain's bridge."

Quickly making up my mind, I climb the endless steps, past the fourteen hundred passengers sleeping in the sun and gently whispering wind, across the captain's bridge with its long, broad window looking out onto the far horizon.

"Captain, I only wanted to ask you if you can land me somewhere in Spitsbergen, some time, somehow."

The captain gravely shakes his head; no, it is quite out of the question. He will, on the contrary, do his best to bring all his passengers back home safe and sound. Besides, you have to get permission from the Norwegian government to stay there over the winter.

"But my husband's expecting me there."

As we continue talking it transpires that the captain knows my husband, has in fact put him off three years before at Kings Bay.

"Of course we won't do anything to prevent your landing," he says. "Let us know when you get your telegram."

With a lighter heart I leave the captain's bridge, hire a deck chair, and enjoy the rest of the journey as free of cares as the other passengers.

We come to the fjords, the typical fjords of the north, glacier-green water out of which grow sharp dark rocks, waterfalls fluttering down the mountains like white banners. Every morning, my bed and toothbrush are lying in a different fjord. The passengers leave the ship, are taken by car to the most romantic spots, jump from stone to stone across the small

25

glacier streams, tease the wild mountain goats, eat their packed lunches, take snaps, write letters, and buy souvenirs.

In the evening we return to the giant ship, vibrating with machinery, the bustle of the kitchens, and comfort. We are fed, bedded down, and carried further. Dancing, flirting, eating, and drinking, we make our way along the famously beautiful coast, until one day we notice that northward the world is growing lighter and lighter, more bleak and more lonely.

The nights do not darken. Bare and craggy mountaintops jut out of the livid light of the water. A strange cool wind blows to me out of this primeval landscape. It might be the world in the last days of the Flood.

Behind the glass doors of the promenade deck, in the illuminated coffee lounge, the people sit around. They smoke, drink, and dance, thinking and talking exactly as they do in the evening in their neighbourhood local in the big city. They do not seem to take much notice of this strange world from which in a week or two they will return, having eaten and slept their fill.

We are in Tromsø. Fishing trawlers and polar ships lie in the harbour, quiet and modest. They smell of tar and fish oil, and they are encompassed by an atmosphere of adventure, of ice and storm and distance.

Today the people of Tromsø have eyes only for the German giant of the ocean; they stroll around the streets and the harbour; there is a tremendous bustle. All the shops are open, although it is ten in the evening.

Asking the way with the address in my hand, I call on a Tromsø family to whom I have an introduction. The road crosses open country, birches and fields and wasteland. Everything here is gigantic and beautiful. The hemlock, nearly ten feet tall, has magnificent flowers, and leaves of tropical luxuriance. The doubled summer light yields double growth. I come to a white-painted wooden villa set in a piece of fenced-in nature. There do not seem to be gardens and parks here. Luxuriant nature is park enough.

The family receive me with open arms. They are the first people who know the object of my journey. Since I cannot speak a word of Norwegian, the daughter-in-law acts as interpreter.

"Papa thinks that if he were you he wouldn't go to the icy wastes of Spitsbergen."

"I'm not afraid," I reply. "My husband thinks it's not very different up there from central Europe, so long as you're warmly enough dressed."

"Your husband is used to the winter," says a son of the house, shaking his head.

They ask if they can be of any help.

"Helmer Hansen knows what I have to get. My husband wrote to him about everything. I must buy what I still need today."

Helmer Hansen is sent for. I imagine him to be a giant. He accompanied Amundsen in the discovery of the South Pole, and was his companion on the northwest passage in the *Gjøa* and on the northeast passage in the *Maud*.

Helmer Hansen is a strikingly well-built, quiet man, with large kind blue eyes. He shakes my hand again and again and says: "Captain Ritter will be glad that his *fruen* is coming." Then he becomes business-like. "*Fruen* must buy *komaga*. You don't need waders, but get felt socks."

These are brought from the town, in all sizes for me to choose from.

Komaga are hand-sewn boots, as broad as punts and made of the softest leather. The tips of the toes stick up, and the uppers come halfway up the calf. I tried the smallest pair: they were much too large.

"Too small," says Helmer Hansen emphatically. He advises me to take the largest pair. A lot of grass is put into your boots; the bigger they are, the better.

At midnight I am brought back to the quay. The white ocean giant lies out at sea as though on a molten sunset. All the lights on deck are burning. It is an impressive sight. The passengers buzz around the deck like moths in the lamplight. They seem to be intoxicated by the twilight, the bright red of the sky and the water, the timeless dazzling sunset that turns soon after midnight into a still brighter dawn. Nobody thinks of sleeping, not till the ship continues its voyage and it grows cool over the sea. The air gradually turns harsh and cold.

The next day there is no land to be seen. The little flag that plots our course on the map is moved north to the waters between Norway and Bear Island. For the first time the ship's orchestra plays during the day, indeed at every meal in the dining room, perhaps to cheer the people up, to keep them from dread of the great lonely island in the northern polar sea.

I am rather restless since I have not yet heard anything from my husband about where to land.

The next day we pass the southerly tip of Spitsbergen. On the eastern horizon, between the shimmering grey sea and a low-hanging curtain of mist, a remarkable strip of land gleams, a strip of blue mountains cut by white glacier streams glittering in the sun: the coast of Spitsbergen.

"Over there lies Longyear Valley, the last outpost of civilisation; it's a Norwegian coal mine," says someone on deck.

Then comes unpeopled land. The whole day through, mountains, glaciers, blue rocks, white ice. At night the land is covered in mist; we see nothing of the north coast, as I had hoped. Early in the morning the ship is due to reach the limit of the pack ice.

Many passengers dance through the night. All the others are wakened at four in the morning by the call of trumpets. Today it sounds different, extraordinarily fresh, quite sparkling, and it brings all the sleepers to their feet. Everybody rushes up to the promenade deck.

Hmm. So that's pack ice. A few timid, dirty-yellow ice floes are lying idly between mist and water. Everybody is freezing. Only the ladies in their elegant fur coats, feeling themselves observed, are in an elevated mood. Disappointed, they all creep back to bed.

The next day everybody sleeps late. The world is wrapped in a thick mist. The foghorn blows unceasingly. The ship is on its journey southward again.

I have made up my mind that if I get no news from my husband I will in any case land at the Ice Fjord. Somebody at the coal mine is sure to know how, where, and when I can find him. But the radio-telegram arrives that morning. "Awaiting you at Kings Bay." It is at once a deliverance from and a cause for anxiety. Will the ship make Kings Bay in the mist? The foghorn is frightful. From the bow of the ship it is impossible to see the stern.

"Purser, will the ship put in at Kings Bay?" He shrugs his shoulders.

"Baggage master, will the ship put in at Kings Bay?"

"You come back home all nice with us," he says.

Anyhow, I get ready and settle the last formalities on the ship. Bored, the passengers stroll up and down in the mist; many of them think of food, but most of them are already in their minds back in their offices at home. I am at least as nervous as the entire crew in the grey impenetrability of the mist. The ship stops. We are at Kings Bay. I jump into the first boat going ashore.

A wooden bridge looms up out of the mist. A handful of men, among whom I recognise my husband. He is the tallest and thinnest among them.

"There you are then," he says, and laughs quietly. He is burnt dark brown and is wearing a badly patched wind jacket, bleached white, and boots leached by seawater.

He tells me we're in luck. A small Norwegian passenger steamer is making its first journey, calling at Wood Bay, and will put us down at our winter quarters. That will save us the troublesome journey by foot across the interior.

The fat old baggage master himself rows my luggage across to the Norwegian ship. It fills the entire boat. My husband laughs. In Europe he would have got angry if I had taken too much luggage on a journey. He has changed in the Arctic. His beaming serenity makes a strange impression. Certainly he is quite different from me and all the other passengers.

He shows me round Kings Bay. With a certain touching solemnity he tells me about everything, but with the best will in the world I can find it neither beautiful nor gripping. The coast is comfortless, bleak, and stony.

"This is the Norwegian coal mine that went bankrupt, and here is the airship hangar of the unlucky Nobile expedition, and over there—you can't see it in the mist—is the little hut where I spent my first winter three years ago."

The passengers stamp around between the deserted wooden houses of the mine and heaps of rusted iron. They are not quite sure what they ought to do here. It is raining, and they feel the cold. In flocks they troop back to the ship; the lights in its warm lounge have a friendly look.

My husband takes me to one of the wooden houses, inhabited by a Spitsbergen hunter who acts as a watchman during the winter. He is lying in bed asleep, with his boots on. A half-empty bottle of brandy is on the table. He wants, I am told, to sleep through the hours of the European invasion. He prefers being alone on his island. Awakened by my husband, he jumps joyfully out of bed, fills a tumbler with brandy to drink to the health of the *fruen* who is going to stay a year on the island. Unfortunately, I cannot understand a single word of his Norwegian speech of welcome.

We board the Norwegian steamer, which arrived in the harbour at the same time as the German ship, and in which we are to continue our voyage. All the crew are on deck. Everybody, from the captain to the cabin boy, shakes hands with me, with a wonderfully frank air of camaraderie. Suddenly I seem to have become one of a large family, admitted among the seamen and the winter residents.

For a day and a night we travel through mist. Occasionally we catch glimpses of mottled ice floes in the water. I am told we are making for the Grey Hook coast, where our hut is, but I have not the least idea in what direction we are travelling nor where we are.

My husband then reveals that there is to be another man with us for the winter. "I don't really know how you'll like the Arctic. Anyway, I don't want to leave you alone in the hut too long, and my hunting ground this year is very big. I've known Karl for a long time. Last year he was stationed at Bangen Hook. He's a fine, decent fellow. He comes from Tromsø and is really a polar seaman, a harpooner by trade. This summer he was already on the way home when I asked him if he wanted to stay on another year up there. He didn't pause for a second, and said yes. He's a fool for Spitsbergen."

"Hallo, Karl," my husband calls out across the ship. Karl comes over. A clean, fair young man, with merry blue eyes. He seems to me about twenty years old. We shake hands and smile at each other. We cannot do any more because Karl does not speak German and I do not speak Norwegian. We are all three in the gayest mood, but each of us for a different reason. My husband is glad that he is going to have a proper household, I because I am looking forward to the fascination of the wilderness, and Karl (he admitted it to me much later) for a very special reason. He is quite sure that in the storms and the loneliness of the long night "the lady from central Europe" will go off her head.

We go on in the thick mist. Grey sea gulls fly quite low. They are quite different from the gulls I have seen until now. They fly with short, powerful beats of the wing. Their blunt, grim heads suggest struggle and tenacity. Their appearance gives me the first glimmering of the relentless nature of the Arctic.

The few passengers on the small ship are of every nationality, but closer acquaintance reveals them all as Spitsbergen enthusiasts. There is a middle-aged English millionaire, burnt brown and scantily clothed. His legs are bare; he wears sandals and shorts and a thin raincoat, which is even shorter than the shorts. He has hardened himself for Spitsbergen. He loves Spitsbergen and has been there again and again in the summer, travelling with the fishermen in their small cutters, studying the land and the people. He intends going there again several times.

My neighbour at table, an Englishman, gives me an enthusiastic account of his cross-country expedition in the spring, which ended with him and his companions losing all their equipment in a rushing glacier stream in the Wijde Bay. But next year he will come again and spend the winter on the northeast coast. "Perhaps you'll stay right on now," my husband teases him. Mr. Glen was already on the way home when he heard of the *Lyngen*'s journey and turned back. He cannot tear himself away from the island.

"Mathilas is buried on Grey Hook," says the ice pilot. "He was a famous polar seaman and took his ship to Spitsbergen when he was seventy."

"Spring is the most beautiful time there," says a young Norwegian with a remote smile. "An unforgettable time…"

"Yes, but I'm not going to let myself be caught by the island, like you've all been caught," I say defiantly.

"Oh, you'll be caught, too," the Norwegian says, softly but with conviction.

So we go on in the mist. Meals are the only break. An attentive steward pushes the best of everything in my direction so that I can enjoy life before it becomes a desert.

It must have been toward the end of our journey when the manager of the telegraph station at Advent Anchorage, an elderly gentleman who seemed completely weatherproof, said to me in a fatherly and benevolent tone: "Madam, if you want to get through the winter well, you must remember three things." He spoke a broken Norwegian German, slowly and with great emphasis. "You must take a walk every day, even in the winter night and storms. That is as important as eating and drinking. Always good temper. Never take things seriously. Never worry. Then it will be fine. I've known Spitsbergen for twenty-five years."

I am grateful for the advice. I know that I will remember his words.

After travelling twenty-four hours through the mist the engines suddenly stop; the ship is still, rocking in the black sea over which the wind moves. "We're there," my husband calls out.

"Do you see your hut over there?" says the young Norwegian standing by me, and points to a spot in the mist. And then indeed I slowly discern in the distance a bleak, grey, long-drawn strip of coast and on it something that looks like a tiny box thrown up by the sea, which must be our hut. All the passengers come on deck and stare with the same gaping repulsion at the coast. As though to show us a last kindness, they help to lower our luggage overboard. Nobody says a word. Only one elderly gentleman, speaking German, finds his tongue. "No, dear lady, you cannot possibly stay through the winter there. It would be quite unreasonable."

But as I stick to my decision to follow the men, he becomes quite angry. "Young people today… it ought not to be allowed… You can't get rich there," he cries at last, quite desperate.

"No, we can't get rich there," I agree.

"Yes, you will get rich," says the young Norwegian, but there is no suggestion of material gain in his gentle smile.

The captain promises to return in a year's time to take me off. They shake hands with us, the captain and all the sailors, in wordless comradeship. Their eyes are eloquent of the seriousness of the moment. "Good winter," they say, as one man, in a last farewell.

But we three are quite boisterous. There is something forced in our laughter perhaps. It would have been easier to get from the rope ladder into the water than into the boat, which is rocking violently. But at last we land safely on the piles of cases and bags. The sailors row off. Slowly we approach the coast.

In our boat sits Mr. Glen, freezing and rattling in the wind and rain, with nothing on his head and no warm clothes. The country has taken all his possessions, but he seizes every opportunity of setting foot once more on the island. "Oh, how I'd like to stay with you," he says. "Spitsbergen is a wonderful country," and with glowing eyes he stares into the mist.

It's a ghastly country, I think to myself. Nothing but water, fog, and rain. It bemuses people until they go out of their minds. What does this island mean to them? What do they get out of it? How many hopes, how many proud plans have been shattered here, how many enterprises met shipwreck, and not least, how many lives has the island claimed?

3

First Days in the Wilderness

We draw nearer to the coast; it is no more inviting at closer range than from the distance. A boundless, dark, flat land, out of which three mighty black mountains rise abruptly, like heaps of coal. Mercifully, they are half-shrouded in mist.

The sailors row us into a small inlet, not far from the hut. They jump into the water in their high waders and drag the boat ashore. I am lifted out like a puppet and swung in a high arc onto dry land. Chests and trunks are thrown out after me.

The Englishman has been inspecting our hut; it strikes him as a palace. He jumps back into the boat and immediately jumps out again to give us a small saucepan of tar and a brush, the remains of his expedition's equipment. This is his parting gift. Karl and my husband are delighted.

Then those who have brought us ashore row back to the ship, lying like a shadow between mist and water.

My husband and Karl heave and shove the luggage out of reach of the surf and, with great exertions, push the heavy chests over the steep rocky shore onto the flat ground by the hut.

How quiet it is here on the island; the beat of the ship's engines is still in my ears. The waves break monotonously on the rocky strand, cold and indifferent. Involuntarily the thought comes into my mind: Here we can live; we can also die, just as it pleases us; nobody will stop us.

The scene is comfortless. Far and wide not a tree or shrub; everything grey and bare and stony. The boundlessly broad foreland, a sea of stone, stones stretching up to the crumbling mountains and down to the crumbling shore, an arid picture of death and decay.

The hut stands in the middle of a small promontory, whose banks drop steeply down to the sea. It is a small, bleak, square box, completely covered in black roofing felt. A few boards, nailed higgledy-piggledy over the felt, provide the only light touch in all the blackness. A solitary stovepipe rears up from the roof into the misty air. Chests and tubs, sleighs, oars, old skis, lie against the walls, and around lie the bones of mysterious animals. The two gigantic skeletons, larger than life, with short, powerful foreleg bones, the jaw of a beast of prey, and human-looking feet may be the skeletons of polar bears. There are a number of remarkable skeletons, with spindle-shaped thoraxes, the pelvis tiny, the legs short and sturdy with long-toed feet... and odd, graceful figures as of cats running. And over all the bones and stones an incessant drizzling rain, soft and quiet.

From a way out comes a triple blast. It is the *Lyngen*

taking a last farewell of us. Then it begins to move off, and its last glimmer dissolves slowly into the mist.

Now we are alone for a year.

You cannot tell the time of day from the overcast sky, but judging from my raging hunger it must be somewhere about suppertime. The men are still busy with the baggage, so I decide to see for myself how, where, and when a meal can be got ready. With some trepidation I approach the little hut. Through the doorway I enter a sort of anteroom, or passage, with a cupboard like a locker, which leads through a very small door with a carved wooden handle into the hut room. It is piled high to the ceiling with nailed-up chests.

"Our stores," says my husband, coming in and pointing to the chests.

"Unpack quickly, children. I've a terrible hunger."

"*Fruen* wants to eat," Hermann says to Karl. Karl scratches his head thoughtfully and sinks into deep meditation. After a brief exchange of words a quick decision is made, and chests, trunks, and boxes are thrown out through the small anteroom into the rain. In the hut there are left only two large sacks, one of flour, the other of sugar, a small case of ammunition, and a few fire bricks, which are handled like sacred relics. Then Karl lights his pipe, takes up a pitcher, and goes out.

"Where's he going now, just when we want to eat?" I ask my husband.

"To look for fresh water," is the laconic answer.

"To look?" I am horrified. "Then you don't know where it is?"

"No, we don't yet know the district round here either. The first time we came here in the cutter to unload our stores, we couldn't stay long. But the hunters say there's a stream here, somewhere, somewhere nearby."

"Somewhere? But suppose he doesn't find the stream, this Karl?"

"Then he'll bring back a lump of glacier ice."

"For cooking?" I am startled. "But is there a glacier anywhere here? You can't see anything in the mist."

"A couple of miles from here at the outside there's a glacier. Karl can get there and back in an hour and a half," my husband says soothingly.

I have to sit down on a small stool. A new way of measuring time begins to dawn on me. My hungry stomach was not prepared for this, and I think with longing of the *Lyngen*, now far from us in the mist, with its tables covered by white cloths, and its sauces and appetisers and the attentive steward. I think of the German ship and its luxurious dinners served automatically on a conveyor belt...

My husband sets about lighting the stove. He does his best to make me feel comfortable. From under the stove he pulls a

little box filled with birch bark. With the bark as kindling, a few sticks of wood, a generous shot of petrol, and a match... the answer is a tremendous bang, and dense black smoke out of the stove door and the pipe.

Hermann draws a dagger from his belt and goes out. He comes

back with a chewed-up piece of bright-pink fat, the yellow rind still sticking to one side. That too is thrown on the fire. There is a tremendous hissing and crackling, and mixed with the new clouds of black smoke a strong smell of fish oil; then the fire goes right out.

"It hasn't been cleaned," says my husband indulgently, and goes out.

I am struck dumb by the stove, and possibly even more by my husband. In Europe he had always been so touchy about soot and about stoves that didn't work. How Spitsbergen has changed him. And it is quite incomprehensible to me how one can calmly tackle such a beast of a stove, on an island where there is no other stove to be got, and in such a thin-walled hut, too, surrounded by storms and the winter night…

A closer inspection shows that the stove is a catastrophe. It is fractured down the middle, so that the four legs stand all askew. It is smothered deep in layers of salt and rust. The oven pipe gapes open and will not shut. There is no ash can at all, but in its place an unsteady dustpan, eaten away by age and rust. There are twelve concentric rings on the stoveplate; at the centre they tumble over each other and make a little hillock.

I can hear Hermann stamping about on the roof, and sounds come from the stovepipe. In the hut the smoke is intolerable, but when I go to open the windows I find that they are not made to open; they are puttied firmly in. So I throw open the door and stand in the rain.

My husband is on the roof, hidden by clouds of smoke and soot. He has tied an old felt hat to an oar and is working it up and down the chimney of the stove. "The stove's all right," he calls out to me. "Nois the hunter told me it's one of the best in the whole of Spitsbergen. You wait, it will soon be very cosy in the hut. Just take your things off and make yourself comfortable inside."

I have no desire to take my things off and make myself comfortable in the sooty hut. I remain sitting in my hat and coat, ready for the worst. But the beast of a stove really seems to be getting a move on, and by and by the pipe even gives out some warmth.

Scarves of smoke trail about the room, which is no more than ten feet by ten, and the soot is settling down on what little primitive equipment there is. I take it in only half-consciously: two broad wooden bunks in the corner, one on top of the other, a plank bed along the wall, a small table under the window, a large shelf and a small one, the latter with some small dusty bottles that seem to contain spices. Outside, about two yards from the window, there is a tall wooden post, bleached snow-white.

"I say, what's that gallows doing there?" I ask my husband as he comes in.

"That's the bear post. It can be seen a long way off, and it attracts the bears from the polar ice to the hut."

"Ah!" It is all I can say or think.

"Yes, and through this little sash window in the wall here you can shoot the bears from the hut. If we're lucky, the pack ice with the bears will come in the autumn."

While talking happily to me, he is bustling around the hut like a housewife who wants to make her guests as comfortable as possible during their visit.

It takes all my self-control not to betray the horror and dread I feel at all the new impressions crowding in on me. I am amazed at my husband who seems to have quite forgotten how a European woman is accustomed to live. He seems to take it completely for granted that I will feel quite at home in this wretched hut, with beasts of prey for company. Anyhow, his way of introducing me to the wilderness does not seem very considerate.

Karl comes back. When he sees the stove burning he rubs his hands happily and cries over and over again, "Fine, fine." The trails of smoke and clouds of soot do not seem to make the slightest impression on him. He has not found the freshwater stream, but instead a lagoon of melted snow water and now he begins to cook. He takes an enormous cast-iron pan from the wall, probably intended for bear blubber, pours in half a jug of water and something from a sack that looks like oats. The fire is fed with fat until the stove is roaring and thundering like an express train. Now and again gusts of even blacker smoke rise from the oven pipe.

Now Karl lays the table for supper. Three aluminium plates alight on the table, followed by knives; in between he stirs the porridge. He accomplishes everything standing in the middle of the hut, rocking bumptiously on the soles of his feet.

"He was trained as a ship's cook," my husband informs me.

"That explains the juggling," I think to myself.

Karl goes out and returns with an entire armful of rusty spoons and forks. He had found them in Kings Bay, on a rubbish dump, he tells us with a beaming smile.

Hermann receives the gift and takes it down to the shore and washes everything in sand and seawater. Meanwhile the porridge is boiling, bubbling, and spitting on the fierce blubber-fire.

With a courteous "Be so kind," each of us gets a ladleful of the boiling porridge on a plate. It is really hot, and since the salt cannot be found, a spoonful of seawater is added.

As we eat we can see from the window a broad expanse of rain, sea, and mist.

"Which way is north?" I ask.

Karl points: "North, south, east, west," and then, like a traffic policeman giving directions in the fog: "Bangen Hook, Verlegen Hook, Jammer Bay, Sorge Bay,* Dead Man's Bay…"

"What is he saying?"

"Those are the names of the neighbouring coasts."

"And we had to winter right here where the coasts have such terrible names?"

"We can rebaptise the coasts if you like," my husband says with a smile.

"Yes, but why did they give them such horrible names?"

"In the spring or summer, ships often get driven by the ice onto these northerly coasts. But the ice can't hurt us. We're on land."

We go on eating and staring out into the mist.

"It's typical summer weather for Spitsbergen," my husband says as though he feels bound to apologise. "It's the warm gulf stream near the pack ice that causes all the fog."

"The weather will get better," Karl puts in, "once the naked Englishman has gone overboard from the *Lyngen*." He insists that the Englishman is looking for a bride in the polar sea. Karl cracks his jokes in spluttering Norwegian.

---

* The English equivalents would be Anxiety Hook, Distress Hook, Misery Bay, Bay of Grief [translator's note].

We eat a great deal of the porridge, but I am not really satisfied. My stomach has been spoilt by the luxurious meals onboard ship. After the porridge we have a few pints of coffee. The Norwegian hunters set the greatest store by coffee, my husband informs me.

The coffee is thin and has absolutely no effect on my desire to sleep. I am dead tired. My eyes are smarting from the unending daylight. I look round for a bed. I am seized by a secret horror of the two bunks with their hard straw mattresses. Who knows what wild hunters last slept there.

"Where is the boudoir you promised me in your letter?" I ask my husband.

"It's not built yet," he replies. "First we have to find planks. The sea sometimes throws them up."

A sailor's kitbag is brought in. A yellow silk quilt, bright as a new pin, is spread ceremoniously on one of the bunks. On top of that, with an "Eff you pliz", is laid a sheepskin sleeping bag. Eff you pliz, I have not the first idea how to get inside a sleeping bag.

My hat and coat are politely removed, and then without hesitation I am lifted up and into the bag and rolled like a joint of meat against the wall. My husband, in a reindeer bag, takes the plank bed, and Karl climbs into the bunk over mine which, close up against the ceiling, looks more like a drawer than a bunk. The boards of the bunk creak and crack under his weight. Will they really bear it?

Although we are all three dead tired, none of us falls quickly asleep. It is as light as day. The alarm clock on the shelf opposite points to two, presumably two in the night. The little bear window is open. Swathes of mist drift in, and softly I can hear the surf breaking. I lie wide awake on my new hard bunk, rolled in the sleeping bag that is damp from the rain and smells faintly of sheep. My glance rests on the men's waders, hung over the stove to dry.

I had imagined Spitsbergen otherwise. Perhaps the fault is mine that I do not like the country. Perhaps I am not over-civilised enough to appreciate the primitiveness here. And then I can't get the stove out of my mind. I could have brought a new stove from Tromsø if I had known. Perhaps there is another hunter's hut somewhere in the neighbourhood with a better stove that we could take. But there is nobody else along the entire north and east coast who would miss a stove that had been removed.

I have to put it to myself as a hard geographical fact, how alone we are up here. Nobody as far as the north pole, nobody across the sea until Novaya Zemlya, and nobody for three hundred miles southward...

The next morning I am wakened by the noise of the little coffee mill. My husband is already up and getting breakfast ready. Karl's feet, in spotless white socks, are dangling from the bunk above. He glances down between them and says, "God morning, Chrissie," and then, slowly and carefully, "Haff you sleep well?"

My husband signals that Karl has just learnt the sentence by heart while I was still asleep.

"I slept very well, Karl. And you?"

My husband corrects me. "You must use *du*, not *Sie*. In Spitsbergen everybody is *du*."

"All right. And you?"

But Karl has nothing more to say. He is in no hurry to learn German, apparently. He cups his hands under a steady drip of rain falling from the ceiling to the floor. *"Fin regn,"* he says dreamily. Then with a sailor's agility he clambers down from the bunk to the table, drinks his coffee and puffs his pipe, watching me all the time. The sight of a "lady from Europe" in the bunk seems quite a novelty to him.

My breakfast is served in bed: oat porridge and coffee, both at any rate quite hot.

"Unfortunately we haven't any bread yet," my husband apologises. "We'll have to bake some. Stupidly, there wasn't any yeast or any baking powder at the store where we bought our provisions. We'll have to invent some kind of baking powder for this winter."

"Invent?" I gape at him. "How will you invent baking powder? You're not a chemical factory. If it could be invented so easily, we housewives would have invented it long ago."

The two men smile placidly. It seems to be a matter of complete indifference to them whether we have to do without bread for a whole year or not. I am revolted by their equanimity.

Karl is eating his porridge in comfort, but suddenly jumps up from his seat as though electrified. For a moment he stares intently out of the window, seizes his rifle from the wall, and rushes out.

Looking through the window I can see him, crouched like a cat, making his way to the shore. Once there, he waves his arms, whistles and twitters in the most enticing tones. My husband, standing in the doorway of the hut, also twitters.

The head of a seal rises from the water and inquisitively approaches the shore. I can clearly see its black smiling face. Slowly it swims nearer.

Karl takes aim and fires. With a comical somersault the seal dives underwater. Stooping, Karl runs further along the shore; then he kneels down, his gun ready. And waits. The seal's head bobs up again. As it swims along, black and wet, it looks happily and inquisitively around. Karl fires again, and again the seal ducks and disappears. I breathe freely.

The men come back, laughing. I hear Karl say, in tones of regret: "It's a pity; it would have made a nice dinner for the lady."

My dear Karl, I think to myself, that's one dinner I can easily do without. I'd a thousand times rather the black old chap were alive in the water than dead in my stomach.

The men are busy outside, and I decide that I can now get on with my morning ablutions.

There does not seem to be much water for washing in these northern expanses, whereas the tin basins that serve for washing are enormous. Then I make my bed, that is, I turn my sleeping bag inside out and hang it on the hut wall, as the men did theirs.

After that there is little clearing up to do. There is no water for washing the dishes, and the only broom I can find has lost all its bristles. In their place some clever hunter has stuck sea-gull feathers. The whole thing is more like an Indian orna-ment than a broom and is no use whatever for sweeping. The worn and rusty dustpan leaves behind more

dirt than it takes up. Apart from three enormous whetstones under the bunk, each of a different kind, and an ice axe, there does not seem to be any more household equipment.

"Tell me," I attack my husband as he enters, "what have you done with all my kitchen things you took with you to Spitsbergen three years ago? You took all my brooms and at least half the cooking things."

"I've still got them all," he says defensively. "For instance the brooms are in the hut at Cape Petermann, I'm sure of that."

"Where is Cape Petermann? Can't we go there and get the brooms?"

"You can't get there very easily," my husband replies. "It's about two days' journey by motorboat. But we're sure to be going there some time this year if the weather's good."

Again I am made conscious of these new dimensions of time and space, and begin slowly to grasp my powerlessness as a housewife on this island.

We unpack. How many days it takes is difficult to say. For here there are no days because there are no nights. One day melts into the next, and you cannot say this is the end of today and now it is tomorrow and that was yesterday. It is always light, the sea is always murmuring, and the mist stands immovable as a wall around the hut. We eat when we are hungry; we sleep when we are tired.

To cheer me up, the hunters take me with them to get drinking water. The way to the lagoon is like a journey into the incorporeal. Mist above us and around us, and under our feet nothing but stones. Large, broken, sharp-edged stones, on which at every step forward the feet slip back half a step. The men find their way in the mist by the stones. Their arrangement, their slight differences from each other, scarcely perceptible to a layman, serve as signposts.

Here is the line of the coast, the line marked by waves on the stony foreshore that in the course of centuries the retreating sea has left behind; here are small heaps of stones, believed to be graves, and here there are wood and bones forced out of the earth by the frost. And if there are no such signposts to show the way, the hunters build cairns, which are stones laid high one upon the other.

"You must learn to find your way around in the mist, in case you have to get water yourself when we're away on an expedition," Hermann says. "You go at a right angle to the stone walls, then left at the graves and parallel to the stone walls, and then straight on till it slopes down to the lagoon."

Stones, stones. Everywhere, sleeping and waking, I see stones. I feel that they are becoming an obsession. The stony land, the whole monstrous barrenness, clings to me like a bad dream.

Europe is already left far behind. It seems to me now like a magic land. Flowers and fruits grow out of the earth there. Out of the earth grows what man needs in order to live. Here, where nothing grows, I grasp for the first time the whole tremendous miracle of eternally growing food.

Secretly, for I do not wish to speak of it, I come to believe that we shall die of hunger here, or at least of scurvy. I have little confidence in our stores. Regarded superficially, it is true, the store cupboard is a comforting sight. Row upon row of boxes, bags, and jars, just like a shop; but when I think of vitamins, they seem very inadequate.

I go through them again and again: beans, peas, lentils—no vitamins; tea, coffee, cocoa—no vitamins; sugar, polished rice, white flour—no vitamins; dried fruits are notoriously dried dead, salted meat salted dead, and condensed milk is said to lose its vitamins in six months. In Europe we have fresh milk every day, fresh butter and fruits and vegetables, all dripping with vitamins, and here, for a whole year, our entire supply of vitamins is contained in a small box of butter, a small jar of honey, a bottle of cod liver oil, and six heads of cabbage. Half of the potatoes are rotten, they must have been stored in a damp place onboard ship; the bilberries do not look exactly fresh, and when Karl unpacked the hundred eider duck eggs that he had gathered in spring on Bangen Hook, we found that seventy-five were broken. "Doesn't matter," he says, "the fox has to have something to eat also," and he puts the box with its huge omelette at the back of the hut. Following a dubious Spitsbergen recipe, I have salted the six cabbage heads, which are meant to be kept fresh till the spring, and hung them in a hollowed-out stump from the ceiling in the passage.

Well, that's the position in regard to vitamins.

"But we'll have fresh meat," my husband says consolingly. "Don't worry; everything seems more difficult in the fog. It's a well-known fact up here. Everything seems easier when the sun's shining. And it really isn't such a pity about the potatoes and bilberries; they were a year old anyhow when we bought them in Advent Anchorage. There weren't any fresh supplies there yet."

"Next year we'll be cleverer," says Karl. "We'll take all our vegetables dry, and instead we'll have two fresh living women."

It is grotesque how carefree they are. Have they no thought for the long night, for the many months when everything will be frozen over? Are they really relying so firmly on hunter's luck? It makes me uneasy to think that, with so few vitamins in our stores, our lives depend entirely on hunting, on what the day happens to bring us; in fact, on accident. The men seem alien beings to me. Is it just levity, or does their serenity spring perhaps from a deeper wisdom that we Europeans have lost?

It seems to me that we have finished unpacking. At any rate, everything has been sorted, stacked, and stowed. I have washed the walls and floor of the hut with soap and boiling water. Under one mattress I found some mildewed men's clothes. Karl gave me a description of the hunter who was the last to live in the hut before us. "Long red hair"—he makes a circling movement round his head—"long red beard with peas and lentils in it, never washed, never shaved." Whereupon I took the mildewed clothes and threw them into the sea.

Now that the whole hut is tidy and I know that it is clean, my secret horror slowly disappears. I see it for the first time with other eyes.

The reddish tint of the smoky walls is pretty, and so are the white reindeer skins on the bunks and bed. The hunters' fur coats hanging on the wall add a stylish touch, as do the Lapp boots and bright belts, the daggers and hunting knives stuck into the beams of the wall. The small stools made of driftwood washed ashore are charming, and the ornaments that the hunters carve in the winter night are touchingly primitive. A small bear nailed to the door, a wooden spoon with a fishtail handle on the little shelf over the table, and in the corner under the ammunition case, in a minute garden of moss, a small carved Madonna, painted once in bright colours but now smoked black, with the infant Jesus on her arm, gazes into the hunter's hut with a soft, tender smile. The layout of the hut is attractive. All the Spitsbergen hunter's huts, my husband tells me, are built and arranged with a wonderful symmetry. They are the product of an uncorrupted sense of beauty that is still alive among these people of nature.

In the evening, satisfied with our day's work, the three of us stand on the large door sill in front of the hut and gaze out into the greyness.

There, quite close to the shore, a seal's head rises again from the sea, quiet in the mist. Karl creeps into the hut for his gun. As though hypnotised, the seal, with its neck stretched out of the water, stares at the hut and at our three figures. "Duck," I say to him in my heart, and hope that it will have some effect on him.

A shot is fired. The seal does not duck. Like a great black balloon he remains lying on the water. "Got him," says my husband, and he and Karl run down to the shore. In a flash the boat is pushed into the water, a few hasty strokes of the oar and they have him.

I tiptoe into the hut; I do not want to see what is now going to happen. But before long they call out to me:

"Would you mind bringing a basin?"

Obediently I take a basin down to the shore. There is the seal, lying on the black stones, already slit up and laid open like a book. Its slender spindle-shaped torso has been removed and is lying on the oval blanket of its skin with its thick layer of pink fat. The entrails are still twitching to the rhythm of the heart's beat.

"Of course he's quite dead," my husband says soothingly.

Karl cuts up the body with a few rapid, incredibly confident strokes of the knife. Then from the fatty skin he removes the small solid little feet with their long flippers and smacks them into the basin.

"We can have that for supper this evening," Hermann says.

Obedient and shuddering, I carry the twitching dish back to the hut. I am utterly at a loss. Ought I to boil, roast, or bake the flippers, and with or without the skin, with the long black nails or without? I shudder when I think that I will have to eat it. They call out to me again. "Another basin, please. Larger if there is one."

I take the big bear basin down to the shore, this time to receive the seal's liver. There are five enormous pieces, weighing at least six pounds.

"You know, the liver's best when it's eaten quite fresh," my husband informs me.

I am very glad that I can now evade the problem of the flippers, and I prepare for the evening meal masses of "liver minute steaks", with mashed potatoes and fried onions.

Faces expectant, noses twitching, their hands covered in blood and blubber, the two murderers, their work done, return to the hut. It takes a lot of hot water and soap to get their hands clean. Then they eat. They eat... I am kept busy filling their plates. They eat until nothing is left of the enormous liver, and then they ask me what I have done with the meat. What have I done with the two flippers they gave me?

I am staggered. "You're like cats, who can go hungry for days and then swallow a whole ox, bones and all."

"Everybody who has to live by hunting is like that," my husband asserts.

Karl has eaten so much he can scarcely move, but he gets up from the table and, bowing in my direction, says "*Takk for mat*."

"What's he saying?"

"Thanks for the meal. That's what they say in Norway to the housewife when they've finished eating."

It strikes me as a very pleasant custom. At least it is cheering for the housewife when she has seen the fruits of many hours of labour in the kitchen polished off in a trice.

We all sleep wonderfully well after the good meal and wake the next day with the strength of bears. It is not for nothing that seals are the favourite food of polar bears.

So today we look for work commensurate with our strength. The two men set about improving the hut. A new sheet of felt is nailed on to the roof and painted with tar. In a great access of courage, I stumble off into the fog, for the first time alone, to get drinking water.

I just follow my nose. After a little way, the thick mist breaks before the black mountains. Seen at close range they are frightening in their vast bleakness. In the great hollows at the foot of the mountains new black mountains are growing, built by the stones which—loosened by frost—fall incessantly into the valley with a soft rattling sound. Today the mountain crests are covered in fresh snow, and the spectacle of these mighty primitive forms, in boldest black and white against a patch of deep blue sky, breathes a vast amplitude and an extraordinary freshness. Then the mist settles again. Suddenly I feel light as a feather. The road over the broken stones is easy to find and soon I am at the lagoon.

Cheerfully I begin the journey back. After a time that seems to me endless I can again hear the sea breaking on the shore. But there is no sign of the hut. I walk a fair way northward—nothing. Twice as far to the south—still nothing. Back again northward, at least three times as far—not a sign of the hut. Nothing but an unfamiliar, black, stony coast, flat, and with inlets that all look alike. Or do they look alike? There is nothing to hold on to, nothing to give direction. A slow sweat of fear chills me; I have left the bucket standing somewhere or other long before this—and there, in front of me, suddenly and quite unexpectedly, is the hut.

The men are still working on the roof. They break into a roar of laughter when they see me coming back, desperate and without the bucket. I am nearer to tears than laughter, particularly when I think of the water I have left behind and that I need for cooking.

Finally Karl shows some sympathy. He jumps down from the roof and goes along the shore to look for the bucket. He is soon back and puts the full bucket down with a bow at my feet.

So the days pass in the mist. The men always have something to work at, and I expend all my European culinary arts on the seal. But now I am at the end of my resources. Whether I boil, bake, or roast it, the meat is always black as coal, and whether it is seal blubber or seal cutlets, the taste is still the same, something between hound and fish. But the men are enthusiastic about my dishes, and I have to cook seal for every meal. Hunters seem able to live on nothing but meat, to my deep sorrow, for I must say I've long grown tired of the black animal.

For me, the seal has rather a moral value. Ever since it has been there, lying ready on the sawing trestle in front of the hut, I can slice off three or four meals from it every day, and like the gift of the good fairy, it never comes to an end; and now I have seen that a single shot will produce an entire butcher's shop from the sea, my anxiety about our vitamin intake in the future is considerably lessened.

It must be about the end of August. In any case, it is getting toward night, for the sun is low in the north. I have just seen Spitsbergen for the first time.

I woke up. I don't know why. Perhaps it was the fresh, clear air, which is like an elixir. Looking out from my bunk through the two open doors I saw, for the first time since I have been here, a blue sea still and glittering in the sun. I crept out on my toes.

Such splendour! We are living on an indescribably beautiful piece of land. Before us a magnificent bay curves in broad arcs away to the north, ending in the open sea. The mountain range across the water is steep and rugged, wildly romantic. A deep blue-green, the mountains rear up into a turquoise-coloured sky. From the mountaintops broad glaciers glittering in the sun flow down into the fjord. The black mountains on our coast lie sombrely in the sun. With their remarkable conical shape and the crests and crevices edged with snow, they remind me of the Japanese mountain Fujiyama, the dead volcano whose massive, simple form you see in so many Japanese paintings.

Many Fujiyamas lie in a row along our coast to the south. As the distance increases, their sombre blackness seems to be lit up by a deep red light. They take on every shade from red to lilac, and all the colours have a glowing depth that is never found in the landscape at home, or at most only in some exquisite flowers. In the holy stillness, everything is lit by a supernatural brightness. Two gulls fly low and silent close by the hut toward the fjord. They are lit up by the red rays of the bright sun. Their magnificent broad wings are a deep pink in the turquoise sky.

Back in my bunk I cannot fall asleep again. I feel as though I have had a glimpse of another world.

At five o'clock I get up. The men are still fast asleep. Today I make my ablutions in the open. The sun is in the east, already high over the black mountains. Behind the hut, where its rays are thrown back by the black tarpaulin wall, it is really warm. I fill the white enamelled tub, which the men fished out of the Ice Fjord and presented to me as a bathtub, with fresh water, and fill a pitcher with seawater down by the shore, and then I have a wonderful bath followed by a saltwater shower.

Never in my life have I felt so intensely, toweringly well and fresh as after this bath in the Arctic sun and the icy seawater.

The hut comes slowly to life. Soon the men appear, freshly shaved today and in freshly washed hooded overalls.

We are all three in the highest of spirits. To celebrate the return of the sunshine we have a whole spoonful of honey with our coffee and cold seal.

Today the hunters cannot bear to stay long in the hut. Soon they are in their boat with their guns, and I must leave everything as it is in my little household and go with them on their short hunting expedition.

The little motorboat travels fast along the black slatey coast. Further out, where the Grey Hook coast ends in a spit of land, we encounter the first black eider ducks. Two are brought down. Then the journey continues. The boat overtakes a whole crowd of mother eider ducks who have gone with their young, only a few days old, for a swim in the sunny water. Mothers and young are spared by the hunters at this season, but they are not spared the most deadly fear. Karl—I could have killed him at that moment—takes the boat right into the midst of the duck families. The little ones struggle anxiously, trying to get out of reach of the throbbing monster of a boat. Like little balls of wool, they rush away over the water with their powerful little webbed feet. But when they see that their quickest pace does not help them, they all suddenly dive, as though at a word of command. Now the old one is quieter. She is not worrying about herself. Tranquilly she lets the boat pass her.

After that the chase becomes more difficult. It is as though a warning wave had spread among the birds, telling them of dangerous creatures along the coast. The ducks rise from the water with a clapping of wings and make off into the distance as soon as they come in sight of the boat.

In the afternoon we return through the sun from our journey. The ducks, fastened two by two to each other, are tied to the bear post, to be dried in the open for winter stores. From three of them Karl removes the skin and feathers. Breast and legs go into the saucepan to be cooked, all the rest is casually thrown away. These birds, I am instructed, cannot be plucked, because the skin, and even more the layer of fat underneath it, which tastes fishy, are inedible; apart from that, offal is of inestimable value in Spitsbergen.

This dish, too, comes out coal black, but the broth is excellent, and the black, tender meat tastes at least as good as the meat of wild duck at home.

Now that the hut is clean inside, I long to get the outside tidied up, too. The disorder is inappropriate to the perfect harmony of the scene. Surreptitiously and quietly, for I am sure to be doing something wrong, I sort the skeletons out from the luggage, the skis, and the empty boxes. But the men have discovered me, and I am read a lecture. "Please leave everything alone; all that untidiness makes the deepest sense. The ice anchor, the ice axe, and the snow boots go on the roof; and everything else is lying just as it should against the wind."

Anyway, I have cleared up so far that now there are at least only stones and bones lying in front of the hut. With a little imagination you might picture it as a newly made rock garden, still without any green it is true.

But I am not to enjoy my rock garden for long. For Karl decorates it with revolting flowers. The next seal to be shot finds a horrible use. Not only is its blubbery skin stretched out on the newly painted wall; no, that is not enough; Karl buries the entrails in little graves that he has dug all round the hut, and then carefully half-covers them with large stones. The skeleton of the polar bear is also lovingly hung with entrails.

"That's to attract the foxes," my husband explains.

Good-bye, my pretty rock garden. I submit to the inevitable.

The next day we bake bread. Not that the men have in the meantime discovered the chemical formula for making yeast; they haven't even thought about it, but they have had luck. In Nois' ammunition chest Karl has found a little box with some stone-hard remains of dried yeast. This is carefully softened and stirred in a bucket with water and flour. The bucket is placed in one of the bunks and warmly wrapped in blankets.

The rough hunters are changed men today. They creep around on their toes and talk in whispers; the door must not be opened; the heat in the room is awful, and all our thoughts circle round the yeast that is to be brought back to life.

At last the dough in the bucket does rise; nursed so tenderly, it rises over the edge and into the warming blankets. The soft sailor's curses grow louder, but on the whole the mood of dedication lasts. We are happy, for now we are saved. The yeast is alive, even on this stony island. We will cultivate yeast, as the country folk do at home, and then oh miracle, old as the Bible and now become for us part of the natural order of things, we shall have fresh bread every day!

And now the kneading, on the little table by the window at which we eat. The hut shakes, and the sweat starts out on the men's foreheads. They are white from flour, and the hut is white. Standing ready on the stove are the bear pans and empty tins, and every available utensil in the hut. A murderous fire is stoked up. Since the oven pipe is not working, the bread is going to be baked on top of the stove, and the hut itself will be the oven.

I flee into the open. Eating cold seal and condensed milk out of the tin, I enjoy the light night. These light nights are strange. A peculiar sanctity rests over them. The waves seem to beat more gently, the birds to fly more slowly—the night is like a dream of day. The welcome smell of baking seeps through the wooden walls into the open.

Untiringly, until morning, the men go on with the baking. Loaves of every shape, light and crusty, are leaning against the window to cool.

Lying in my bunk, tired out, I can hear the end of the bakers' day. Sailor fashion, a bucket of seawater is poured into the hut, and the floor and stools are scrubbed. Fresh air flows in through the open doors, and all three of us sleep deep and well.

The next morning we have bread for breakfast. We eat bread with butter, bread with cheese, bread with seal, bread with salted bacon. What a delight it is to bite once more into fresh bread when you have had none for a long time. In Europe, with its abundance, nobody has an inkling of this joy.

After breakfast Karl takes his gun, shoves the boat into the water, and goes off. "He's going to cross the fjord to Cape Roos, to inspect huts on the hunting ground over there and to set bait for the foxes. He'll be away about eight or ten days."

"But why hasn't he taken any food with him?"

"He has his gun," my husband says with a smile.

We walk eastward toward the glaciers; here, as on all our walks, we meet practically no living things. Here and there a little flower grows between the black stones, a soft-yellow silk poppy on a hair-thin stalk sways in the wind, sometimes also a timid crowfoot. My husband, who has for years seen nothing but stones and ice, waxes enthusiastic about the "vegetation", while I am untouched by the sight of the flowers. I eat them all up and pretend to myself that they are vegetables full of vitamins.

Once we come across a fly, buzzing low over a little hillock of moss under the dark mountains, seemingly anxious not to lose its way in the wind and the vast space.

4

Mikkl

He stands on the heap of refuse, with an air of the utmost naturalness, rooting about among the empty tins. His snow-white silky fur, the kind of fur you see in Europe only around the necks of elegant women on festive occasions, seems quite out of place on the garbage heap. But he allows nothing to disturb him in his unappetising occupation; he seems deeply preoccupied and does not deign to look at the three of us on the door sill, staring inquisitively.

For all hunters it is a great moment when the first polar fox pays his first visit in the autumn. These foxes, particularly the young ones, who are ignorant of the hunters' intentions, often display great attachment to human beings and come running to the huts practically every day.

This fox, too, the men maintain, will become a *hüsrev*, a house fox, for he is still quite young and cannot yet have had any bad experiences.

In form and colour he is like a white Pomeranian, not very large, and differing only in having a long, bushy brush. The ruffle of fur around his neck makes his face look round; he has large dark eyes, small round furry ears, a tiny, black-pointed muzzle and carmine-red tongue.

Karl twitters to him in Norwegian, calls him Mikkl—the Norwegians call all polar foxes Mikkl—and throws down small pieces of cheese in front of his paws. He calls him by the sweetest names, and at the same time casts an expert eye on his fur; Leif Anders in Tromsø, he imagines, will hardly give thirty kroner for him.

"Then don't kill him," I implore the men. "I'll give you the thirty kroner in Europe. Let the sweet thing live."

Vanished are my dreams of one day owning a white fox fur. Now that I know what a live polar fox is like I no longer want a dead one. Mikkl shall stay in the beautiful, wild homeland where he belongs.

"Mikkl's fur will become quite beautiful when it gets colder," my husband asserts.

"No, no," says Karl disdainfully, "it will always be pure muck. The hair on the back is too short, and the grey spots on the fur won't go away either."

Thinking that I have found an ally in Karl I add at random: "Besides, his brush is too long and the paws are too short; a lady would never wear anything like that." I steal a look at Karl, but he avoids my glance and only looks enquiringly at my husband, who looks away. Now I see that there will have to be a hard fight between me and the hard-hearted men if I am to save Mikkl's young life.

"Poor Mikkl, you don't know that your hosts are fox hunters. Don't be a fool; go away from here, go to another country where there aren't any people."

Mikkl looks at me. He looks me straight in the eyes. His

whole beautiful little face smiles; he has not understood a word I have said. Mikkl, who is now our constant guest, seems to find his way around very well. He jumps from one delicacy to the other but eats only a little of each, just like a gourmet. He buries his white muzzle deep in the refuse bucket and drags out from among the ashes and potato peelings the entrails of a fowl, which he swallows by the yard without once biting them through. Then from the garbage heap he scratches out the ancient skin of a bird, shakes it a few times round his white muzzle, and then eats the lot, feathers and quills and all. "Good vitamins," Karl observes.

Mikkl is very suspicious of the odds and ends that are thrown to him. When Karl is skinning a seal, Mikkl stands quite close and follows every movement of the knife. If some of the offal is thrown to him he takes to his heels and prefers to gnaw at the ancient skeleton of a bear. But he cannot resist freshly killed eider ducks and gulls; he carries these off at full tilt.

On all our walks Mikkl now accompanies us like a faithful dog. Wherever we go, he suddenly turns up but acts as if he were not accompanying us, but going his own extremely individual way. Now and again he creeps behind stones, as though stalking birds. He also plays a genuine game of hide-and-seek with the hunters among the large stones, ducking and peeping and yelping with joy when he outwits them. And then quite suddenly, it may be, he breaks off the game and runs away without even turning round.

The white polar ptarmigan, which used to be seen in large numbers near our hut gathered around the leavings of food, have become more cautious since Mikkl appeared on the scene. While the rest eat, one of them always mounts guard, keeping watch from a raised position, usually the roof of the hut. If the sentinel rises from its post, all the others fly away too. There is no gull to be seen far and wide when Mikkl is in the neighbourhood.

For some time Mikkl has had a blue friend that he brings with him now and again. The blue fox never comes on his own. We are all under the impression that "Blue" is anxious to warn Mikkl against us. Just as Mikkl is trustful—he almost eats out of our hands—so the blue fox is mistrustful. He always stands a bit further off. As soon as he catches sight of one of us all his hair stands on end. He stands stiff and tense, his eyes wild and flashing with fear, like a hyena.

Now when we go walking, Blue often turns up too and tries to entice Mikkl away from us. But Mikkl is stupid and remains stupid; he goes on trusting human beings.

We also have a third house fox, but this one comes only at night. It is a gluttonous blue vixen that has discovered behind the hut a box of old, rancid margarine that had belonged to the hunter Nois and we had thrown away. Night after night I hear rustlings and rattlings outside the wall by my bunk, and every morning about four packets are missing. The blue vixen is growing noticeably fatter; her fur is luxuriant and gleaming, "first quality", as Karl says.

The men are packing boxes and making great preparations. I still do not understand their Norwegian, and when I question my husband he is evasive. But a little while ago they asked me quite formally whether I can shoot well. So we had some target practice with rifles, and to my astonishment, I hit the bull's-eye at fifty paces. Thereupon they asked me what I would do if a bear came to the hut when I was alone there.

"I'd put a saucer of honey for him outside the door."

"That's what I thought, that you'd be so stupid," my husband stormed at me. "If you don't want to shoot, you must stay in the hut and promise me that you'll never offer a tidbit to a bear."

So I promise, and then I am offered the choice of accompanying them the next day on their journey into the interior, or staying alone by the shore.

Of course I want to go with them on the trip.

After all the preparations are made the weather suddenly changes, and gales from the north rage for days. A journey across the sea by boat is unthinkable.

5

By Boat into the Interior

A few days later, with a suddenness that is quite usual in Spitsbergen, the wind dies away overnight. As the barometer reading is favourable, we decide to start early on the journey across Wijde Bay, to carry supplies to the huts on the other side and get them ready for the approaching hunting season.

With magical swiftness the two hunters have finished all their preparations for the journey and made our hut secure against storms while we are away. The boat is lying in the limpid waters of the little inlet. It is loaded high with a jumble of boxes containing food, sleeping bags, tools, guns, roof felting, window glass, stovepipes, and a skinned seal to provide food for the journey.

"When the weather is at its best, squalls are on the way," runs an old Spitsbergen weather formula, and that means that we must lose no time when the weather is good.

After a quickly eaten breakfast the window shutters are closed, the hot ashes raked out of the stove, and a few heavy posts propped against the door.

In the forepart of the boat a regal couch of quilts and sacks has been arranged for me.

As our small motorboat chugs along in the sun over the broad expanse of water, making for new scenes and seas, we are seized by an over-brimming sense of happiness in our worldwide freedom, in the complete absence of any restraint.

Soon we can survey the entire north coast and the Norway islands. Today the stretches of coast with the terrible names— Bangen Hook, Jammer Bay, Verlegen Hook, Sorge Bay—are smiling in the blue sea, shimmering in sunlight, clothed in the colours of summer. The water is so still and clear that in its depths we can see the shining greenish sunlit ribs of rock and cliff, and dark forests of seaweed whose branches reach up and touch our boat. Where the rocks rise out of the water, hundreds of great white gulls are dozing in the sun.

After we have passed the tip of Grey Hook, Wijde Bay opens up before us. Arrestingly beautiful, it dreams away its remote, untouched existence in quiet and sunshine. For hours we journey down the immense fjord, which stretches inland for over sixty miles. We keep to the west bank, now close under the high wall of cliff, now further out because of the banks and shallows that extend from the estuaries and deep valleys. To the east a fabulous coastline accompanies us. Sharp-edged rocks of primeval granite alternate with glaciers rushing down to the fjord, and above the curiously shaped mountains rises the lofty, glassy shield of ice that is New Friesland.

My husband tells me about the journey he made with Governor Ingstad the previous spring by dog sleigh in a raging snowstorm over the icy slopes of New Friesland. Karl stares dreamily at a single spot. At the foot of that mountain in Mossel

Bay lies Bangen Hook, the place where in that same year he spent a winter with his seventy-year-old comrade Anders Andersen of Tromsø, a wrinkled little man who managed to pass himself off as ten years younger than he really was in order to get permission from the marine supervisor's office to spend one more winter of his life as a trapper on his beloved Spitsbergen.

Following the directions of the builder of the hut, we discover our first refuge in a charming bay at the foot of a dark overhanging mountain. Hunters have an acute sense for scenic beauty in choosing the sites for their huts. Of course they have to consider the proximity of fresh water in making their choice and a suitable spot for mooring their boats. We are all three greatly astonished when, the next moment, the hut seems to have been blown away. But it reappears, as though out of a trapdoor, and we can make out the doors and windows; then it completely vanishes again.

"It's a ghost hut," says Karl, shivering comically.

Having landed, we hurry up the steep bank, and now we understand. Instead of a hut there is only the timber framework of a hut. There is no question of our using it as a refuge. Either time or planks were short when it was built; the hunters often have to bring the building materials for their huts from a great distance, taking many days in their rowboats. We do no more than set bait to attract the foxes in the neighbourhood of the hut to the traps.

To the whole bay, which is still unnamed on the map, we give the name Spooky Bay.

The next huts, which lie along the coast at distances of four to eight hours' travelling, are the strangest and historically the most interesting in all Spitsbergen. At one time such huts were to be found all along the coasts of the island; now they survive only in Wijde Bay. They were built about two hundred years ago by Russians, who were the first hunters to spend the winter on the island; among them were Russian monks from the Solovetsky Monastery. One of these monks, Prince Starachin, spent thirty-two years on the island as a hunter. Tall wooden crosses still bear witness today to the services they held in the open. Their graves, on little tongues of land commanding a wide view, can be found all over Spitsbergen.

The Russian huts are timbered throughout with strong driftwood trunks, carried down the Siberian rivers by the current and cast ashore here. The wood is bleached white by years in the sea, by the wind and sun and ice. Because of their weight, the huts have sunk deep into the ground. In that immense stony land they look like small pale doll's houses. Grass grows on the flat roofs, and among it there is a gleam of blue clay. The hunters brought the clay with them from home. It is said to be still quite impervious to rain and snow.

The first Russian hut we investigate, called Torenhüs, is half-buried under sand drifts. The small window has been broken by a bear, and the bunk is covered in seaweed washed in by the spring tide. The stove has fallen to pieces. Here, too, we do no more than set bait around the hut.

As we continue our journey the west coast grows steeper and steeper. We pass high walls of rock from which facades like colonnades jut out, the clefts between cut by the heavy seas. Gulls accompany our boat for hours and the seals come so close that we can hear their breathing. The hunters are in a most peaceful mood. They are singing and not thinking of their guns.

Our next objective is the notorious Villa Rave. The hut does not deserve the name of villa. It is a wretched structure of roof felting built onto the ruins of a Russian hut set in the middle of a bleak spit of land and surrounded by puddles and driftwood; for here too, when storms blow from the north, the sea invades the hut. The door has been crushed in by sand drifts, and the inside of the hut also shows signs that the ice has penetrated. A small window set crookedly into the wall gives just enough light to reveal the fantastic desolation. The black walls cave inward, pressed by the masses of earth heaped up outside. The bunks, placed obliquely to the wall, are covered with mildewed reindeer skins. Grotesquely arbitrary in shape, everything in the hut is smoked black. The whole interior suggests a sick man's vision of horror.

But that does not deter the men from choosing precisely this hut for a long midday rest. Karl fetches some pieces of ice from a nearby lagoon for water and a sawn-off slice of seal from the boat. While I cook, he tries to spoil the last remains of my appetite with his stories.

The hut has the reputation of having brought misfortune on every expedition. Death and scurvy have their stubborn habitation here. One woman who had spent the winter here died in the boat on the homeward journey, and a member of an important scientific expedition had left his frozen big toe here. Here, through this hole in the roof, a bear was once shot in the winter night.

To my immense disgust, the hut is considered to be quite fit for an overnight stay during the winter expeditions and, should the onset of bad weather make it necessary, for longer periods also. Boxes of stores and sleeping bags are brought in and good cooking utensils hung on the walls.

Taking advantage of the windless weather, we continue our journey. The sun is following its shallow course behind the mountains in the west, and the magic of the bright Arctic night surrounds us. Once more it seems to me a miracle that the evening twilight does not fade on the horizon, as it does at home, but slowly, little by little, again ascends, trailing with it over the mountains a streak of pastel-blue night. The blue light pours over the strange landscape, giving it the serene tenderness and solemnity that all things take on up here in the bright night.

Sheltered from the wind by the southern foreshore at the next hut, hundreds of sleeping eider ducks, like a large black island, are swaying on the water. Slowly they swim out of the way of the boat. At this time of the year the birds gather for their flight south. The male birds have already left Spitsbergen, soon after the hatching of their young. The females go south in the autumn. The young remain in the north through the winter night.

In its quiet abandonment, dwarf-like and white, the little Russian hut at the foot of a dark precipitous mountain, transfigured by the magical light of the blue night, no longer bears any resemblance to a human habitation. After we have removed the heavy tree trunks from the small door of the hut, we creep on all fours through a small anteroom into a still smaller living room in which none of us can stand upright. The whole thing is like a small, low, black burial chamber, but the hunters are enthusiastic about the heat of the oven and the cosiness of this hut on winter expeditions.

We make tea on the most primitive of stoves that can be imagined. It is in fact nothing but a tin bucket resting on stones and fitted with a pipe. A bent frying pan serves as stoveplate.

The rest of the journey by boat I spend asleep in my fur sleeping bag, and only awaken when the hunters, with intentional violence, let the boat run aground onto a new beach.

I can scarcely believe my eyes. A radiant red dawn illuminates a land that is itself red. Red is the sea, red the rocks, red the beach, and the square driftwood hut is tinged with red.

This is red desert sand, sand from the earliest ages of our earth, I am told in answer to my question. Completely dazed as I already am, even without this, by the orgy of colour in the scene, the picture they paint of what happened on this once desert expanse makes me dizzier still. Here, within the earth, tremendous forces have been at work, transforming desert sand into mountains over inconceivable ages of time, while more than once the land was submerged by the ocean and re-emerged.

Beside the pink hut there is a tiny garden, planted perhaps by a homesick hunter with gathered moss and weeds. Here the little wild garden, no more than a yard square, is miraculous, an exhilarating spot of green in the immense redness.

Meantime Karl, who does not allow himself to be bewildered either by colours or by geological images, has been in the pink hut, making some glaring red cocoa. "I had to make the cocoa so thick," he says apologetically, "so that you would not see how red and sandy the water was that I had to make it with."

We continue on our way. After about twenty hours of travelling we near the end of our journey. In the cool of morning the entire fjord has been covered with a thin layer of ice, which the keel of our boat shatters into thin slivers with a soft jingling sound. Triumphantly, the sun rises over the horizon, irradiating a superb scene of precipitous, bright red cliffs, the arms of the two fjords of Wijde Bay, into which the mighty Mittagleffler glacier streams down. Here the highlands of New Friesland are broken into countless sharp groins and ridges projecting from the glaciers.

There in the fjord is the small island of Corspynthen—Cross Point—only at times connected with the mainland by a narrow strip of sand. The graceful Arctic terns that rest on the island fly whirring round our boat. At the entry to a large, sandy red lagoon over whose sunlit waters innumerable white and black seabirds are circling, there is a small, idyllic bay where we land.

Weighed down and walled round by heavy lumps of slate, the little hut where my husband spent last winter lies close to the rocky shore. Within—and this is perhaps the greatest surprise of the whole journey, here in this most remote corner of the fjord, where it was least to be expected—we find an extraordinarily snug, well-cared-for little house. Through the small window with its red-striped curtains the sunlight falls on a small table covered with a cloth, on a comfortable bunk and a small sofa. On the walls, papered in light brown, hang maps, a barometer, and field glasses. And on the narrow windowsill by the table there is a framed photograph of our small daughter.

We sit with our steaming coffee, gazing at the lagoon, joyously alive with birds, the mountains glowing red in the background. Then, partly on improvised beds made of planks and doors taken off their hinges, we sleep our well-earned sleep after the long journey. The sun-filled air comes in through the empty doorway of the hut, and now and again the cry of a bird and the thin call of a sandpiper. We spend some days on this small romantic island with its magnificent views. On the red desert sand grow small, pale-yellow and lilac flowers. Among them lie reindeer antlers covered with moss and the gigantic skeleton of a whale, which in the course of the centuries has become porous and white. On the highest spot of the island there is a grave and under the small wooden cross the deserted nest of an eider duck.

Here lies buried one of the most daring hunters, whose deeds have taken on an almost mythical character in the stories told of him today. He once crossed alone from King Karl Land right over the frozen waters of the Olga Strait to Spitsbergen. A long while after that he died on the small island in the fjord with, so it is said, a curse on his lips.

The hunters repair the traps in the neighbourhood of the island and gather wood for winter fuel. On the first morning of our stay, returning from their trip in search of fresh water, they bring back their boat filled literally to the edge with meat. On the way they had shot a bearded seal—a large seal, weighing over eleven hundred pounds. The liver alone filled a large bucket, and another bucket was filled with its blood.

Karl cooks some blood pancakes, a speciality of Spitsbergen hunters, and with great gusto eats practically all of them himself, while we only nibble at little morsels of the delicacy, feeling compelled to eat some because of its high vitamin content.

The sun shines, the stove works well and has an oven. I have found everything I need for baking a cake, and so we three live on the little island as in fairyland, luxuriously and free from care.

There is only one thing wrong with the place: the weather changes even more suddenly than it does elsewhere in Spitsbergen.

One day, when the weather is at its clearest, we row over to the west fjord to look for a vanished boat that was flung by a storm last autumn from where it was lying close by the hut, across the beach and into the fjord. We row across the water, which here and there is as red as an opaque dyeing mixture. After a two hours' journey they put me off at a small hut at the tip of Cape Petermann. The men are extremely surprised to find the hut still standing; it might quite easily have been washed away by the glacier stream nearby. I am to look for fresh water and get a snack ready while the men continue along the coast in pursuit of the boat.

I take a kettle with me on my search for water. The glacier water is too red and too sandy for boiling.

I pass by dark mountainous cliffs and overhanging cornices of red glacier ice. In every direction impassable glacier streams block my path. Far or near, there is no drinking water to be found. On my wanderings I espy, sticking out of the reddish sand of a glacier stream, a fragment of blue-striped linen. I fish for it and gradually pull out an enormous piece of linen, which on closer inspection I recognise as coming from my own linen closet at home. Later I learn that this bedcover served my husband as a sail; it had been rigged to the vanished boat. Quite close to where the sail was found I discover a small eddy of clear water, a freshwater spring in the glacier stream.

I make tea in the half-flooded hut, which is in fact only held together by the enormous tree trunks leaning against it on every side. The bunk is suspended over a foaming pit, and so is the small table, on which a candle is calmly stuck. The stove is still on dry ground. There are saucepans hanging on the walls and crockery on the shelves.

Then I sit down in front of the hut and wait for the men to return. Around me towers the massive, desolate, rocky landscape. The stillness of the air is torn by the wailing cries of a small white gull that is being driven hither and thither high in the air above me by a parasitic Arctic tern. The hunters give the name of *tyviu*, thief, to this satanic bird, which never seeks its own food but chases the solitary flying gull.

Along by the entry to the fjord a low bank of cloud comes into view. Quickly it moves nearer. But here too come the two hunters along the shore, the boat found, and they leave me in no doubt that we must hurry home before the storm breaks. The tea is left untasted.

But we are no further than the middle of the fjord when the wind comes whistling along. Banks of mist roll low over the water, meet and unite against the cliff walls, and rise threateningly upward. The red sea becomes agitated. Wave after wave surges up from under the impenetrable wall of fog. The wind increases rapidly in strength. The two men set to work with a will, and the water pours down their faces. Karl in his leaking boat has to bale more than he rows. We in our heavy boat can scarcely move against the sea and wind, and the fast-running current. But we are in front of the shallow mouth of the Landingsdalen River. Here, and for a long way out, the seas are breaking heavily. Shall we get by, or will the storm drive us in?

At last we have to give up; we can do no more. The harsh, steep beach that we are making for is scarcely fifty yards long. To right and left of it tall cliffs jut straight out of the sea.

The two boats are lying close together. One wave after another rolls under them. The men are keeping them out on the water, every muscle stretched. A tremendously heavy sea rushes toward us, the men row as though possessed, and riding the crest of the wave the boats slide with a crunching sound into land. In a flash they are torn sideways, and the next sea throws them high up onto the driftwood.

"That went off pretty well," says Karl, and lights his pipe. Then the boats are drawn up higher between the rocks and the moss, and turned over. There they will have to stay until the weather improves.

We have no choice but to make our way home on foot. We are wet from the sea, and the mist is oppressively heavy. We scramble along the great screeds, often over boulders as high as ourselves, the raging waters below, and above us the driving mist. Once again I have the feeling of ant-like smallness in this tremendous expanse of country, and I get a faint idea of the hunters' difficulties on their autumn expeditions.

Through the Landingsdalen, a labyrinth of shallow river mouths, we have to wade. Imperturbably good-humoured, Karl discovers a way of jumping over the branches of the river, which makes not only himself, but us too, as wet as possible. Like a boisterous child he splashes slap into the middle of the puddles. When at last we have crossed the river, which is nearly two miles wide, we are spattered all over with red clay.

The wind dies as quickly and astoundingly as it rose. The restless waters of the fjord grow smooth again. The mists disperse and it begins to rain. Now the fjord is lying in a leaden stillness. A bearded seal is resting on the quiet water, sleeping at its ease in the now placid air with its nostrils sticking up out of the water; in its tropical passivity it resembles a hippopotamus.

The next day the sun is shining again, warmer and more penetrating than at any time that summer. The men go over to the west fjord and bring back the boats. No sooner are they back than the weather changes again, and for two days storms rage from the south.

The fjord is foaming and surging round the little hut. Every now and again the spray sweeps, rattling against the window. Now it is really snug in the hut. The little oil lamp is burning.

"This is the first time the lamp has been lit," say the hunters, gazing mournfully at the light. It must be a great moment when in these vastnesses the lamp is lit for the first time, but I cannot join in the sentimental solemnity, for at home in Europe there is nothing special about lighting a lamp.

My husband talks to us about the solitary winters he has spent on this island. He tells us stories about the hunter Björnes, his neighbour, who spends every alternate winter on the opposite side of the fjord. Björnes, a faithful and solicitous comrade, would often row across the fjord, even in a stormy November after the winter darkness had fallen, to bring his neighbour fresh ptarmigan for winter supplies. Once my husband hunted a mackerel shark that in the last twilight of November he mistook for a seal. He rowed out after it. Fortunately his first shot got home, otherwise the ensuing struggle might have been really dangerous, for the shark could have overturned the boat with one blow of its tail. He tells us of the sleigh dog, Siri, which in the ice-cold night the previous year, about Christmastime, dropped a litter of eight puppies in the nearby kennel. We are given the whole romantic story of this small storm-whipped island in the fjord.

When the weather clears again we decide to return as quickly as possible so as not to be caught here by the equinoctial storms, of which Karl, shuddering, speaks more and more frequently.

This time the only load we carry in the boat are planks from a torn-down shed that are to be used to build a small room for me. On the return journey, not far from the Villa Rave, we are overtaken by a heavy long swell, the aftermath of a storm at sea.

But the air is leaden still. Karl predicts a great storm and suggests that we break our journey. But I implore them to continue, for I do not want to spend a night in the horrible Villa Rave. It would be better to capsize in the storm, swim through cold water, and make our way home by foot over the stony land.

The rest of the journey is cheerless. Every outline is distorted by mirages. The land looks as though it has been overrun by the sea. Karl's cheerful singing is silenced, and he has run out of tobacco; I am half-seasick, and my husband nearly falls out of the boat as in the twilight he sounds the water for shallows. Then in the heavens, among the bright hues of twilight, the first star glows. The first star after many white nights.

The men become sentimental, but I get only more seasick.

With the strong swell it is difficult to get through the reefs around Odden on Grey Hook. We send up a prayer of thankfulness when at last we jump from the boat into the water at the familiar Grey Hook beach. The heavy breakers make it impossible to reach land dry-footed. We find the hut just as we left it, except that the onions we hung out have sprouted and are now curling over the window like creepers.

6

The Earth Sinks into Shadow

For a whole month now we have had day and night in their right order. But now the days are quickly growing shorter. In fact they are nothing more than dawn and twilight. The sun rolls like a fiery ball across the mountains. Now and again, when it is passing behind the mountain crests, it peeps forth again on its shallow course from the gaps between the mountains. Our shadows are yards long, and as we go about our daily work in the open, they make us aware of the great eventide of nature.

We have our hands full and feel that we are being driven by the last rays of the departing sun.

The ptarmigan leave the mountains for the valley. When the hunters catch sight of them descending, they rush out with their guns into the dark valley. We need more birds for winter supplies. The ptarmigan apparently do not stay over the winter in Grey Hook; they are only on their way through, seeking an area richer in vegetation. And so they must be caught when they come down here to Grey Hook to rest awhile.

It would be hard to spot the ptarmigan if one did not see them dropping down. With their speckled black and white protective colouring they look so like the ground itself, where the black stones are now covered here and there with snow, that they can only be recognised from two or three paces away. The birds are intelligent enough to remain "stupidly" still when a pursuer draws near. You can walk through a field of stones thickly strewn with ptarmigan without noticing that they are there. Only at the most critical moments does the bird rise and make off, light-winged as a gull.

For trapping the foxes, too, there are a great many preparations to be made. The hunters cut hundreds of "matchsticks", that is, long sticks to which the bait—the heads of birds and eider ducks—is tied. When the fox tugs at the bait, then the structure collapses and the wooden frame, weighted with heavy stones, falls on the head of the fox, killing him outright.

In the midst of all the rush, my little room has been finished. With double walls, lined inside with thick pink paper, and with a double floor, filled in between with ashes, it is as tight as a bottle. It is only six foot by four in size, but it has got everything, a bunk, a large shelf, a small table, which reaches from the bunk, under the window, to the opposite wall, and a drawer fixed up as a washstand. The little room is charming and welcoming. The low, broad little window looks out southward to the mountains, and the minute stove gives out a pleasant warmth. Spitsbergen coal has the quality of fusing into a lump, which burns the whole day.

When I have time, I use the last of the light and run along the shore to collect birch bark, which makes excellent kindling for the stove, and which a kind fate sends in on the tide from God knows what part of the world for the poor winter dwellers.

Every kind of souvenir of tragic happenings lies there on the foreshore. The planks of boats and lifebelts, with the names of the ships almost obliterated by water. One small plank I found bore the still easily legible inscription: "Cpt. Nobile."

I gather up everything that might be useful, even washed-up clothes. Here everything is valuable. Karl collects the pieces of raw rubber that are still cast up here from ships sunk during the world war. He uses them to reinforce boots. Not long ago he proudly brought back two table legs, apparently of mahogany wood, which he is going to use for carving.

But the one who is driven hardest by the last rays of the sun is our little Mikkl. He makes only brief and hasty appearances at the hut. His collector's zeal verges on mania. He drags everything that is not firmly nailed down off to his earth, and not only edibles. Not long ago he carried off the bamboo pole and its thermometer. Even the fox iron intended for him later, he has dragged off with a great clanking.

Mikkl is collecting for the winter; he has not yet grasped that here everything is designed for his death.

Again and again I ask the hunters if there is not, after all, a way out that will spare Mikkl's life. Karl is of the opinion that we will have to construct a trap that will catch him alive. But then he will have to be kept the entire winter through in the hut, to prevent him from falling into one of the traps set in the hunting ground. Karl once caught a live fox on Jan Mayen. He says it is a laborious job to keep a live fox. The two men do not want to be held up by special tasks; time is running short and they want to have both the large hunting fields covered before darkness sets in.

Mikkl now demonstrates his attachment to us by sleeping close to the hut throughout the night. He lies curled up on his bed of straw with his bushy brush over his nose. The sleeping, shining-white fox fits in wonderfully with the stillness of the night, which still remains magically bright. Mikkl is like a frag-ment of the mysterious Ice Age, lying hidden in the frozen, quiet brightness. In the transparent heavens the large moon looks quite near, not as it does in Europe where its light is cold and distant. Here it seems to belong to our world, the luminous picture of a sharply outlined ice landscape.

Mikkl's behaviour takes on a touch of timidity. All animals grow timid in the winter night, the hunters say. Now he often creeps about like a cat and shrinks away when he is called. But whenever I go to the lagoon for fresh water he turns up some-where along the way and patters along beside me.

"Poor Mikkl, you're traipsing to your doom. In a few days the fox-trapping will begin; they're after your life. They will pull your beautiful fur over your head and send you far away to a place where a lot of people live close to each other. There they will give you glittering eyes made of glass, and then you will hang in one of the thousand glittering shops in one of the thousand glittering streets, together with thousands of other glittering dead things. Do you know, Mikkl, there's so much artificial glitter there that the people no longer know anything about light, about its coming and going, and about the magic of twilight."

I fetch water from the lagoon; it is so clear that I can see the rust-brown weeds at the bottom. Mikkl also laps up some of the clear water but without letting me out of his sight. Suddenly he raises his head and stares at me as though it were the first time in his life he had seen me. Horror glares out of his wide, glowing green eyes; then he leaps aside and runs off without once turning round. He runs across the black field of stone and at last disappears, a tiny spot in my sight, at the foot of the great black mountains.

Perhaps they become clairvoyant, the animals, as the darkness grows, and then see the true face of men?

Once, while the men are indoors carving, I stand on the door sill and look southward where the sky is growing light. For days it has been hidden by cloud, but now it is lit by the most wonderful dawn. It is twelve o'clock midday when the sun rises. It rises half over the horizon, and then sets again and disappears. Only slowly and with a shudder do I grasp that this is the terrible moment when the sun has shone for us the last time this year. I run indoors to the men.

"That's right," they say calmly and go on carving. "It's the sixteenth of October today, and the sun won't come back to us before the twenty-fifth of February."

I calculate that the night will last one hundred and thirty-two days.

The conflict between the weakening light of day and the triumphing light of the moon creates bewildering contrasts in the very clear, violently bleak landscape. New scenes appear whenever the sky lightens.

Today the heavens are shining in the blue light of the vanished day. In the north a red-yellow moon stands out against a bank of fog. Like the reflection of a distant conflagration, the northern lights, growing steadily more visible, drift in subdued reddish gleams across the sky. Moonlight and Arctic light are warm and glowing in contrast to the cold blue of the sky. The moon lights up Cake Mountain (the name we have given to one of the three Grey Hook peaks whose shape resembles a *guglhupf*, the round and fluted Austrian cakes). But the spur of the mountain stretching in front of it is in shadow. It looks as though the jaws of hell had opened behind the shadowed mountain wall, outlining its massive bulk with a diabolic glare.

These are scenes not made for human eyes. The drama of the polar world sinking slowly into shadow is played out in utter silence and remoteness. The scenes are changed by sorcery.

In this freakish twilight the driftwood washed up by the last storm, which we are out to gather quickly before the snowstorms come, seems whiter than ever. White Mikkl leaps about behind us, sniffing at every piece of wood that we have touched as though it were something to eat.

The smaller logs, some of them dripping wet and heavy as lead, some porous and light as paper, we throw to Karl, who accompanies us in the boat close by the shore. The large trunks we saw up and roll into the water, where Karl takes them in tow.

Karl is working peacefully in the boat, taking no notice of the bewitched light, or not wanting to see it; good-humoured and easygoing, he sings his favourite song:

> My wife is far from slim,
> She has every kind of fault;
> She has large hands and feet,
> And her teeth are missing—
> But she is mine.

Punctually on 20 October, the day set for fox-trapping to begin, the two hunters start out along the fjord for their hunting ground to set the traps. I go along with them. Imploring and beseeching, using my entire stock of feminine coquetry, I manage to carry the hunters past the first ten places, which seem to me to be dangerous for Mikkl. But at the freshwater spring they call a halt. Here the first traps are set. Now I will go no further with them. The hunters wave me a friendly farewell with their repulsive bouquets of impaled heads and ask me to return here tomorrow about the same time to take "him" out of the trap. "Carry him in a rucksack and hang him up by the hind legs in the passage."

Hopelessly sad I return home. I have no appetite for any kind of work in the hut; going to sleep is distasteful, and even more distasteful waking to the dark morning. The wind is muttering, the sea roaring, and I think of Mikkl dead in the trap.

As the twilight-dark day grows a little lighter I set out with a rucksack for the freshwater spring. It is heavy going. Gusts of snow chase across the sea; the surge of the sea is tremendously strong. "Unmerciful nature! Unmerciful life!" I think to myself over and over again. Near the freshwater spring I notice in the snow the recent marks of a fox. Of course! Mikkl is sure to have come here to drink water, and as the view clears for a moment I see a white fox in the trap. The trap clearly has not fallen as it should; I can see from a distance that the fox is scrabbling around in the snow with its paws in an attempt to get free. I race along on my skis, but when I get there everything is still; only the wind is playing in Mikkl's hair.

I cannot bring myself to take him out of the trap, to disturb him as he begins his last sleep. I stand there a long time. One gust of snow after the other blows over the quiet trap.

I look out over the agitated sea and the snow-swept fore-shore. There! Am I dreaming? Can it be? Mikkl is still breath-ing—it is horrible. I have no gun to put an end to his suffer-ing—why don't the men come? They would know what to do. But there is no movement on the broad white land. If Mikkl starts scratching again, it means there is enough life left in him, then I will get him out of the trap...

Mikkl starts to scratch again, although a little more feebly. I rush to the trap, tear away the heavy stones, and lift the frame. Mikkl raises his head. He is unhurt and looks at me with an indescribable expression. I speak tenderly to him, but the horror does not fade from his eyes. He seems to be thirsty. I rush home as fast as I can to bring back some warm milk. Oh, how completely the world has suddenly changed. The surging of the sea has in it something joyous and powerful, as though filled with a new life. Little Mikkl is alive.

When I get back to the trap Mikkl has gone. But my husband is there. "I thought it was something like that," he says. "So you did save his life. I saw him running inland along the fjord. Of course he gave me a wide berth."

The next day I confess to Karl that I let Mikkl out of the trap. He laughs. "His fur wasn't good. It doesn't matter a bit." Soothingly he adds: "Mikkl won't get into a trap again. He'll become the oldest and cunningest fox in Grey Hook; he'll have a hundred children."

We never saw Mikkl again.

7

Alone in the Hut

I am alone in the furious drumfire of a hurricane. I think these are called blizzards in books about the Arctic. In any case I have never been through anything like this in Europe. From within the hut it sounds as though an express train were being driven without pause over iron bridges and through screaming tunnels that have no end.

For nine days and nine nights the storm rages without respite, and the worst of it is that the men are away. The storm broke a few hours after they left. I hope to God that they reached the Villa Rave safely the first day. The barometer was unpromising when they went off. But this expedition had to be made, come what might, before total darkness set in, to lay the traps in their hunting ground.

I had just woken up when my husband called in from the door. "We're off now. We can't wait any longer for good weather. We'll be back here in thirteen days, but don't worry if we're away longer. If the pack ice comes down while we're away and a bear comes near the hut, shoot him. It's best to hit him in the breast, and even if he looks as though he's dead, shoot him again in the head. We've left ammunition for you out on the table. And keep the place warm so that the fox pelts sweat, and take temperature readings."

They went off. I heard the long-drawn sounds of their skis as they moved away from the hut. Then everything was silent. Out of doors the twilight was still grey. Snowflakes whirled down thickly from the sky. I was glad that I did not have to go with them and went quietly back to sleep.

When I awoke, toward midday, it had grown still lighter. Now and again powerful gusts of wind rapped on the walls of the hut.

The wind rose rapidly. Beneath its shrill whistle I caught the deep, hollow undertones characteristic of the storm. No, it wasn't the right sort of weather for the two of them to be out in. I thought with a shock of fear of all the things out of doors that had to be secured against the storm. I dressed quickly and, without giving it much thought, dashed out of the hut.

Never had I seen Spitsbergen looking like that. The entire country was in an uproar. The snow was driving like a broad stream of water over the land and over the hut and in clouds over the black sea. The swell was going out seaward. High above, the storm was booming like a deep, long-drawn organ note.

The window shutters were already buried under snow. I had to shovel them out and put them in the passage. The skis, however, were rammed down in a spot sheltered from the wind. The boat was lying obliquely to the wind, already half under snow. Sticking up through the snow I saw large stones; that meant it had already been secured against the storm. The thermometer showed minus ten degrees.

There was not too much fuel in the hut. I set about chopping the sawn logs that were lying against the wall of the hut. From the stories the men had told me, it seemed that a storm like this could last three weeks. I chopped away for dear life. Although protected from the wind by the hut, the work was no pleasure. The flying snow whirled in my face and into my anorak, which in my haste I had not fastened and which now stood up round my head like a frozen pipe. At last I threw all the wood I could find into the hut, following it up with the axe and the chopping block.

Then I set about getting breakfast. But the beast of a stove would not burn. There was a lunatic draught that blew out every flame. I had to use a great deal of patience, paraffin, and seal fat before the fire at last caught. And then it was the same old story as in every storm. The heat whistled out of the chimney, while reeking fumes of smoke blew into the hut. It was pitch-black night out-of-doors before I had a cup of hot coffee in my hands.

The gale was still increasing in violence. The hollow, roaring undertone had swelled into unintermittent thunder. Now and again I could hear the first dull rumbling blows of the approaching storm at sea beating on the cliffs. It was cheerless in the hut. The stove smoked and, although stoked high, the room remained cold. The wind whistled through the wooden walls and the hideous foxes swung gently. In spite of my fur jacket and fur hood I froze, and the margarine blue vixen, one of the first to fall victim to its greed, had stopped sweating.

I wondered how long it would be before this raving northeast storm drove the pack ice down to our coast. Would the polar bears come on the first ice floes to drift this way? Karl thought so. Should I perhaps sew curtains for the window, so that at least I would not see the bears if they peeped into the house? It might restore a feeling of snugness to the hut to do a little job like that.

At once I started looking for the blue-striped stuff, the sail retrieved from the west fjord, and hastily began sewing. But my hands were stiff with cold and black with soot. To add to it all, my little lamp went out. So there I was in darkness, in the midst of that diabolic scene. I felt around for the paraffin bottle; I found it, but it was empty. As far as I could recall, the cask of paraffin was kept out of doors, somewhere between the hut and the foreshore, and the paraffin was funnelled into the bottle through a tube. But I had no desire to set about this in the dark, and who knows if I could find my way back to the hut.

So I sat on in the light reflected from the stove. I thought of what the dreadful fate of a hunter's wife would be who had to spend a whole winter alone in a hut without any light.

There was a young woman from north Norway who accompanied her husband to Spitsbergen. In the autumn the hunter rowed across to the other side of the fjord to set his traps and to pick up a cask of paraffin deposited there. Then the drift ice was carried into the fjord and he could not return. Only in the spring, when the ice was frozen hard, could he make his way back on foot. During the winter darkness his wife had given birth to a child, without any help, and the child was living. It had grown into a sturdy little baby, but the long night and the fears she had endured had left the mother deranged in mind.

The fire burnt down quickly, and what could I do in order not to burn still more precious fuel, but go to sleep? I felt my way into my little room. It was ice-cold, and I crept fully clothed into my little bunk. But it was easier to think of sleeping than to fall asleep, for here the noise if anything was still greater. To the crashing thunder of the storm was added the knocking and rapping of all the boards and posts leaning against the east wall. The wind was howling in the stovepipe, and on the roof the frozen corpses of the skinned foxes, left up there for heaven knows what reason, were tapping and knocking.

Could a storm like this lift the hut from the ground, I wondered? If not, why should all these huts be weighed down with great logs? Did not Karl tell me the story of a hunter who spent several days lying on the floor of his hut because he thought the storm was going to carry it away? The huts are not set into the ground; they just lie like boxes on the stony surface.

And the storm was still rising. Soon it was impossible to distinguish one noise from another. All were fused into a deafening roar. I conjured up a picture of the two men, struggling ahead in the raging wind and darkness along the rocky shore of Wijde Bay, which seems to have no end, making wide circles round the broad lagoons. And when they reach the Villa Rave, would it be under water? When storms blow from the north the waters flood up to the hut.

But in spite of all my anxieties I at last fell fast asleep.

In the rattling hut I awake early to darkness and to the same thundering storm. By the light of a match I look at the clock. It says eleven. And as I raise the small curtain I see that the window has been snowed up. The rest of the hut, too, is in pitch darkness; all the windows are thickly covered with snow.

The stove plays up again when I try to light it. My fingers are almost dropping off from cold before I manage to get the fire going. There is no snow in the buckets to cook my breakfast with, so I put on my boots and anorak to make a dash out-of-doors for some snow.

I open the door of the hut... but what is this? In front of the hut there is a perpendicular curtain of snow. Just at eye level, however, there is a small peephole, and through it I can see a magnificent spectacle. The air is filled with whirling snow, and snow and seawater dashing against the coast rise high into the air. High and foaming white, the breakers roll shoreward.

Snow drives into my face through the little peephole, reminding me that I had come out to collect some snow for making coffee. Thinking to knock down the apparently thin barrier of snow in front of the door with one blow of my fist, I find that I have hit a massive wall. The snow barrier turns out to be about ten yards wide, a ridge of snow sloping gradually down to the foreshore. It is not a very delightful discovery; however, it does calm my fears. There is no chance now of the hut being blown away, nor can the bears simply come in through the door without further ado when they scent food.

I have an abundant breakfast and draw up my plan of campaign. Whatever happens, I have to go out to get coal and paraffin supplies into the hut. Following my plan, I begin by enlarging the peephole in the snow with the coal shovel. Unfortunately, I have to carry indoors all the snow I shovel out. Then, when the hole is big enough to stick my head through, I look first of all nervously toward the northern horizon. Thank God, there is no *islysning* yet to be seen—an "ice-blink", or reflection—which means that the pack ice is not yet within visible distance. I become more courageous. I force my shoulders through the hole cut in the snow and try by twisting and turning to get the rest of me through. Then, head first, I slide down the snowdrift, crawl a few feet further, and reach the pile of wood where the sacks of coal are also lying. It is impossible to stand up—the wind is too violent. So I crawl around on all fours to get into the shelter of the pile of wood, out of the wind. Having done this, I try to drag the top sack from the heap, but it is frozen fast. No wonder, for the spray from the breakers reaches this spot, and now and again I get a smart volley of ice-cold seawater in my face. At last, when I have exerted all my strength, the sack begins to move, but the bottom of the sack, frozen stiff, rips open, and the coal falls into the snow.

Among the sacks I notice a bottle of paraffin. Happy over this precious find, I stick it in my anorak pocket. The next sack is looser; I manage to get it down but, bent over as I am, I cannot drag it after me. Then I remember having seen a small old Nansen sleigh leaning against one of the walls of the hut. I could make use of it now, so I crawl back on all fours to the hut. On the way I notice the handle of the snow shovel sticking out of the snow. Burrowing with my hands, I manage to dig the shovel out.

There is no chance of reaching the rear wall of the hut, where I guess the Nansen sleigh is. There the storm is like a wall, which makes it impossible to go forward. So I take my chance and begin digging on the west side, for there I am sheltered from the wind. The snow heaped up here is light, the shovel is large, and soon the door of the hut is clear. Then I dig a ditch alongside the wall and discover all kinds of treasures—two bottles of paraffin (and now I remember that they were placed there for just such an emergency as this), small sticks of wood, logs, and finally the Nansen sleigh as well.

Unfortunately it is badly knocked about. In the hut I find tools, but it is not easy to knock in nails when you are wearing gloves frozen stiff. I have to summon all my strength to stand up in the storm, and use all my energy and skill to hammer one nail in straight.

At last I get the coal into the hut, crawling along like a dog on all fours and trailing the sleigh behind me. By that time it is nearly night. The battle with the stove starts up again when I set about cooking dinner. Time and again I have to throw open all the doors to let the smoke billow out. And when at last the dinner is cooked and I sit down to my meagre meal, it has become pitch black outside and the hut is utterly cheerless. Like sand in an hourglass, snow is drifting visibly against the small windowpane; I draw the small curtains I have just sewn across the window, but the cheerlessness remains in the hut. Outside storm and surf are pounding, and the sharp wind blows through the walls.

And so it goes on for days, immutable, without a break, the fury of this insane music.

After a while my hands begin to tremble. I catch myself creeping softly about the hut, doing all my jobs slowly with measured movements, as though trying not to attract the attention of the raging deity outside.

Confronted with such an Arctic storm, every human being becomes primitive again, small and full of foreboding. The vengeful gods return. Conscience awakes and hurls itself at men like a monster.

But at night I am calm. I think of my child at home, and it gives me peace. Night after night I think what I must do to hold out against the storm. I must not idly watch the snow rising slowly above the hut. Every day, whatever the cost, I will shovel the snow away from the door, if only so that the men can reach the house when they return tired out from their long trip. And also, as often as I can, I will chop wood and build up fuel supplies.

Slowly but surely the snow rises round the hut. Behind the hut, in the direction from which the snow is coming, a snowdrift is growing, firmly modelled and hard, like a steel wave about to topple over the hut. Every day I shovel a new path through the snow in front of the hut. Each time I try out a new way. Once to the south, once to the west, but each time the path has been snowed up by the following day, and the white wall confronts me as I open the door.

Then I try something else. From the heap of wood I drag some planks to the hut and ram them in along one side of the path I have shovelled out. I go at the work with all my bodily strength in the insane tumult of the storm. For the first time in my life I experience the joy of struggling with something stronger than myself. But the labour is all in vain. The next day the hut is more deeply buried in snow than ever, and I have to dig a tunnel more than a yard long before I can get out of the dark hut and into the light of day. The snowdrift passes over the roof and stretches far down to the sea. For good or ill I have to wrench the heavy planks out of the snow again to save myself from being hopelessly buried.

And so I go on working day after day, during the hours when there is still some dusky light out-of-doors in the storm, with a strength that I did not think I possessed, with a kind of savage recklessness, which seizes me afresh each day. Each morning I feel the same almost trembling craving to rush out to do battle, until one day, suddenly, the storm ceases, and a new experience makes an even more violent and terrible impact on my excited mind than the days of furious storm.

For the first time I realise that in the solitude of an all-too-powerful nature things have a different meaning from that we attribute to them in our world of constant reciprocal relations between man and man. It dawns on me that in many cases it may be more difficult for a man to retain his ordinary humanity in the Arctic than to sustain his life in battle with the elements.

8

Peace After the Storm

Overnight it has become dead quiet, and as I open the door of the hut in the early morning, for the first time there is no white wall. The narrow path through the snow is still there. It leads to a vast, solemn stillness, to a never seen and unimaginable world of splendour and beauty.

It has become quite clear. A lofty, greenish-blue evening sky arches over the snowy landscape of the fjord. Like a shell opalescing into its own shadowy hues, the earth is floating in transparent space, in which light from distant fountains stirs and floats to and fro. Low on the eastern horizon there is a round, bright pool of light, bluish-pink in colour, the reflection of the sun, now slowly circling the earth far below our horizon. We ourselves live in shadow.

But it is as though things up here have acquired a light of their own, as though they themselves emitted rays of the most beautiful and mysterious hues. All the mountains, tremendous in the foreground and sharply edged in the distance, are glassy-bright with rigid ice, glass bright the foreland and glass bright the cliffs along the shore that, transfigured by frost and surf into high, round domes of ice, drop steeply into the sea.

The fjord is as calm as though it had never known a storm, reflecting in its waters the bright silver disc of the full moon. Slowly the light from the distant sun circles the horizon. A few long-drawn shadows, stretching far over the mirror of the waters, pass lightly beyond the fjord. They seem to be skeins of the eider duck mother birds, perhaps the last to leave this high northern inimical world. But to our little peninsula come swimming a host of the young eider ducks deserted by their mothers. Where were the little birds during the frenzied storm that turned the coast into a solid block of ice? Did they find shelter from the elements, or did the elements halt their fury before these young lives? How do the wheels of the vast natural order engage, leaving to each his own? Infinitely peaceful is the sound of the birds' gentle "go, go, go"; how calmly they come swimming in the radiant evening, approaching the unknown fearfulness of the winter night.

I myself stand forlornly by the water's edge. The power of this worldwide peace takes hold of me, although my senses are unable to grasp it. And as though I were unsubstantial, no longer there, the infinite space penetrates through me and swells out, the surging of the sea passes through my being, and what was once a personal will dissolves like a small cloud against the inflexible cliffs.

I am conscious of the immense solitude around me. There is nothing that is like me, no creature in whose aspect I might retain a consciousness of my own self; I feel that the limits of my being are being lost in this all-too-powerful nature, and for the first time I have a sense of the divine gift of companionship.

With an effort I return to the hut, fasten my skis, and go to the distant foreland. I move because I have ordered myself to move, but I do not feel that I am moving. I am as weightless as air. And I cast no shadow on the strangely glowing surface; my feet leave no tracks in the porcelain-hard snow.

And so I go on almost without consciousness, without any familiar object to hold on to, through the vast solitude, through the radiant twilight that has no shadows, through the unmoving timeless quiet.

The regular, too-loud creaking in the air scarcely penetrates my consciousness; I can hardly make the connection between the noise and the movement of my wooden skis; far more alien still is the high clear cracking of the frost.

Then I reach the height with a wide view that I set out for. There they are, the distant coasts, Bangen Hook, Verlegen Hook, Mossel Bay, like shimmering white mirages in the dreaming blue-grey of sea and sky. But further to the north the colours dissolve, and over the sea, still as glass, rises the profound darkness of the winter night.

Scarcely do I dare to throw a glance at the last of the mighty Grey Hook mountains, behind which Wijde Bay stretches to the south. That is where the men made their way, eleven days ago, in the great storm. Their tracks have long since been snowed over. Everywhere, as far as the eye can see, there is nothing but the hard-frozen outlines of the torrent of snow.

If the men were to come back now, I would see them as tiny black points at the foot of the steep white mountain, and very slowly they would approach the immense surface of the broad foreland. But they do not appear. The broad white plain remains empty and quiet.

I turn round and make my way home. Rushing downhill across the stiff frozen ground, exerting all my energy to master my muscles, I at last find myself again, and consciousness of life streams through my heart and limbs.

Only now does the comical aspect of my little house strike me. In the snowstorm it has acquired projecting baroque cornices and bulges. The white snow facade no longer bears any resemblance to a house—it is much more like a large, artistically folded table napkin. The remarkable structure is lit a bright yellow by the vanishing light of the western sky and stands out sharply from the pure lilac blue of the flatter foreland.

Then I creep into the hut. Still blinded by the magnificent brightness of nature, its interior seems to me small and dark. Like the scenery for a human habitation in a bizarre and grimy theatre.

Stoking up the fire, clearing away the ashes, fetching snow, sweeping the floor—these jobs bring back a sense of reality. But entering up my diary presents me today with a hard nut to crack. Why have I been so shaken by the peacefulness of nature? Because it was preceded by the titanic storm? Do we really need the force of contrast to live intensively? It must be that. For a gentle song would not shake us if we had never heard a loud one. We human beings are only instruments over which the song of the world plays. We do not create ideas; we only carry them.

I have a better understanding now of what my husband meant when he said, "You have to be alone in the Arctic to know what living in the Arctic really means." Perhaps in centuries to come men will go to the Arctic as in biblical times they withdrew to the desert, to find the truth again.

. . .

When I look out of the window early next morning, the frost panes are glimmering in the silver light of the moon and in every shade of night blue. Another glorious day of peace, pitched in a twilight key, but the colours are different. Everything is enacted in tones of the purest blue. There are tiny waves on the sea, which is washing the black stones out of the snow along the shore. The coastline, drawn indescribably fine, separates the cold blue of the snow blanket from the transparent green-blue of the mirroring fjord.

To paint this landscape would require the devotion of the old masters. Perhaps this habit of devotion will one day be recaptured. Then the painters too will paint differently. Then the heavens will again become bright and transparent, and all the earth and everything born of the earth will again acquire their firm, clear-cut outline, and only that which has soul and life will carry the inner light.

Today I make all kinds of disagreeable discoveries in my household. During the recent cold days the condensed milk has frozen. The tins in which the milk is still liquid I place, wrapped up in blankets, in the men's bunks. The potatoes are also frozen. They are covered with a layer of ice and shine like Christmas tree decorations. There is nothing to be done about them except to bury them out-of-doors in the snow so that they will not thaw out prematurely. The worst discovery of all is that the seal meat has disappeared. The last time I noticed it, it was hung in front of the hut from three posts rammed into the ground. A fox could not have reached it, and there hasn't after all been a bear. It could only have been blown down by the storm. So I start looking in the snow. I clear a deep furrow down to the foreshore, following the direction of the wind. Nothing. All the stars have come out and I am still digging.

I am really desperate. The seal represented our meat and our vitamins for the winter. What will the men say to their wretched cook who let the food freeze and the meat disappear! But as I go on digging, now quite close to the hut, my shovel knocks against something hard. A few black bristles stick up out of the snow. I shovel out a round black head and a neck, frozen as hard as steel. It is nothing but the tattered remains of a seal long since devoured.

Great as the three food shocks were, they made no lasting impression on my mind. Perhaps I have already acquired the fatalism of the men. Is it the influence of nature in the Arctic that changes men? Does one know here, more clearly than elsewhere, that everything goes its prescribed way, even without man's intervention?

The next day I am aroused suddenly from sleep. I can hear the scraping of rapid, long-drawn ski strokes out in the snow. Have the hunters already come home? I listen, but everything is quiet again. Nothing is stirring. Nor, when I step out of the hut later, can I find any trace of them in the snow.

What could it have been? An hallucination? I had looked at my watch, and it said nine o'clock. If the men had really been able to keep to their schedule, despite storms and bad weather, they might have started on their journey home at nine that morning from their last station, the Villa Rave.

I cannot get it out of my head that the men are coming. They must have been speaking about me, and I, the only receiving station up here, must have picked up their thoughts. In eight hours, I am certain, they will be back.

I stoke up the fire and make the living room warm, melt snow, and give everything a high polish to welcome them. Out-of-doors, it is still night-dark. The moon is shining clearly, but in the south clouds are piling up, and a long slow swell rolls onto the foreshore. Everything is covered in freshly fallen snow, and I sink knee deep in it when I go out to collect some.

I bake a large loaf and, as a special treat, prepare a dish of potatoes, turnips, and bacon. The two of them have had to dispense with the pleasure of fresh vegetables for a long time. Toward midday, as it gets a little lighter, I go out and up to the point that has the widest view over the plain, and from there trace out with my skis clear tracks down to the hut, as a greeting to welcome them.

But as the day goes on the barometer falls rapidly. The sky clouds over, and the wondrous colours slowly fade. The wind comes in northward from the sea. But I still keep the hut warm. Behind the stove I put slippers and I see that dry clothes are ready. I melt masses of snow ready for water to wash in. I try my hand at baking fresh rolls; using leaven of course. On the stoveplate I build an oven out of the lid of a round tin and fire bricks, covered with a frying pan.

So, slowly, it is five o'clock. I sit by the stove knitting, waiting for the two men who, according to my reckoning, should be here at any moment. Water for coffee is bubbling away.

The hut is now really cosy. The two small paraffin lamps give out a pretty light. The new small blue-striped curtains are drawn across the window. On the table, spread with a cloth, the gleaming coffee cups are ready, and one shell with sooty butter, and another shell with a sinfully large portion of honey. And in the middle the highly successful, freshly baked crusty rolls.

But out-of-doors it is stormy. I draw back the small curtains so that the lamplight falls on the snow in front of the window, to guide the men as they approach the hut. In white tatters the snow is driving through the darkness. I could almost find it in me not to wish that the two are on their way.

Six o'clock, seven... at eight I give up hope. With a heavy heart I make up my mind to eat alone; I have not eaten anything yet today.

I stoke the fire high with wood, to heat up the food. There! A violent gust of wind, billow of smoke out of the stove, and the hut is full of black smoke and soot. I fling the doors wide open and stand there, where I can breathe.

Outside the night is pitch black. I can hear the wind raging over the distant snowfields, in a song that rises and falls. It stirs the loose snow lying upon the hard, frozen snow below, and roaring over the hut whips the hard, frozen pellets onto the roof and walls. The sea is singing loudly around the small peninsula.

Suddenly I hear a strange loud ringing sound in the air. It is like the single peal of a bell, deep, full, and vibrating. As though spellbound, I stand there and strain my ears. Will the strange sound be repeated? But everything is quiet; only the wind and water roar.

It could not have been a delusion. I had heard it only too clearly. It could not have come from anything lying about the hut. It came out of the air. This single strange note, metallically

CHRISTIANE RITTER

pure and clear as it was, had something frightening in it here, in this dead land. Perhaps Spitsbergen is haunted, as so many people say it is. Perhaps here you can hear things that you cannot hear in other latitudes, at another level of consciousness. In the darkness I stand in a kind of icy calm, but my brain is working feverishly. What could it have been? Is there no answer to the riddle? I am still keeping terror at bay.

I cannot go back into the hut. The smoke is still billowing out, barring my entry. Then I hear it, soft at first, but growing steadily louder—just as I did this morning—the scraping of rapid, long-drawn ski strokes in the snow. "Chrissie ahoy," rings out to me through the darkness.

I start awake as though from a bad dream. The men are coming home! It must have been their call that sounded so metallic. Its echo had reached me unrecognisably distorted by the wind.

The two dark figures stop, high up on the fresh snowdrift in front of the hut. They laugh. "Heavens, what does it look like here! It must have been snowing pretty hard." They jump down; they come into the hut, covered with hoarfrost, bearded, heavy and stiff and cold. They turn me toward the light and look searchingly into my face. "As a matter of fact we were a bit worried about you. It was your first snowstorm, after all, and you were alone."

"And you went on in the snowstorm? I can't understand how you did it."

"Of course we went on! Didn't we promise you to be back in thirteen days?"

"And early this morning, at nine o'clock, you set out from the Villa Rave. I heard you."

"That's right," they say smiling. They are not greatly aston-ished at my acute hearing; they have had the same thing happen to them often enough.

Soon the hut is no longer recognisable. In the twinkling of an eye it is smothered in wet clothes, boots and socks, and a heap of frozen white foxes. The first thing the gentlemen want to do is wash and shave. They have not taken off their clothes for eight days.

"Mushinka, bring this! Mushinka, bring that!" I scurry around, from cupboard to washstand, from boiling water to snow, from stove to table. I seem to myself like a canary, which after a long flight out-of-doors recognises its cage and hops joyously from one bar to the next.

I am in my own world again. Although only a cook in a sooty hole, housekeeper for two wolfishly hungry ragged men, still I am again a human being among human beings.

"You stupid girl! You dumb cook...!" Ah, how sweet it sounds. Now I know again who I am. Now I have my bound-aries again.

The celebration dinner lasts for hours. Karl devours rolls and honey. "There ought to be a woman in every hut who waits for the hunters."

"A different woman in every one of course," Hermann teases him.

"Well, Svalbard would be lovely then." Svalbard, or "Cold Coast", is the old Norwegian name for Spitsbergen.

Then the two pashas lie down on their bunks and talk to me while I wash the dishes. "On the trip down Wijde Bay we had the wind at our backs. We flew before the storm like flies. For a long time we didn't get into our bunks, for in the night the water flooded right up to the hut. But at last we fell fast asleep and didn't wake until three the next afternoon. By then it was too dark to go on. Next day we got up early, but we had to wade through a stretch of ice-cold water in the darkness because the hut was surrounded by water."

"And where were you then on that beautiful calm day?" I interject.

"In Corspynthen. We shot a bearded seal there."

"On that divinely solemn day?"

"Yes," says Karl enthusiastically. "It weighed at least half a ton."

How varied are the experiences one lives through in the Arctic. One can murder and devour, calculate and measure, one can go out of one's mind from loneliness and terror, and one can certainly also go mad with enthusiasm for the all-too-overwhelming beauty. But it is also true that one will never experience in the Arctic anything that one has not oneself brought there.

The blizzard has started again with all its old force, but in spite of that we all sleep wonderfully well. The storm is no longer frightening now that the men are back. I sleep in my little room as royally as if it were a ritzy sleeping car in a softly sprung express train rolling through the countryside.

9

Night Falls

Days of general relaxation follow. The foxes the men brought back are skinned. The pelts are stretched, with the skin outward, on long, pointed boards. This is to give them the fashionable length. They are hung from the ceiling to dry.

The men rest from their long trip. They lie on their bunks, reading by lamplight; the lamps now burn all day. I often go for my daily walk alone. Usually I choose the direction inland by the fjord, southward, where the sun has disappeared, and where, in four months' time, it will shine again for the first time.

The world is in deep twilight, a perpetual twilight from which it can no longer emerge. There is no wind, and a transparent mist carries the waves of the last dying light. Everything, near and far, is unreal, without spatial dimension. The frozen mountains soar up into the dark-grey sky like white shadows. Weightless, they seem to sway.

With a soft musical note, the dark water nestles in the round white bays and in the river estuaries, and glides in the calm obscurity over to the broad sea, which in the distance seems to melt into the grey of the sky.

The scene has nothing earthly in it. Withdrawn, it seems to lead its own self-contained life. It is like the dream of a world that is visible before it takes shape as a reality.

We call them Chinese landscapes, these scenes that remind us so strongly of the delicate, wonderful paintings of the Chinese painter-monks, in which the immense and mysterious effect is achieved entirely by gradations from light to dark grey, by forms indicated rather than outlined.

If it was the most profound immersion in nature that provided the Chinese masters with the inspiration for their sublime pictures, here it is the approaching night which, stripping the landscape of all its accessories, brings out only the innermost essence of nature itself.

Almost we expect the scenes to dissolve into nothing before our wakeful, critical gaze. But they persist in their magic radiance for hours and days. It is this persistence in timeless light and indescribable quiet that makes the world up here so unreal.

It is difficult to convey the impression made by walking among these mysterious scenes which spatially, it is true, are large and powerful, and in which the human being looks like a tiny piece of dead coal.

Now I accompany my husband on practically all his trips. And whether we go along the coast, along the gigantic Grey Hook mountains, or up the rocky valleys to the glaciers, we are always stirred by new pictures that rise up, gleaming and still. I wonder why we have never heard of these pictures formed by mist in the Arctic. Has nobody who has spent the winter there thought them worth mentioning? Have they never moved anyone before? Has it been of no interest that these Chinese pictures come to life on this island of mist, in a thousand variations?

Why has so little been written about the great transition stage in Arctic nature which, after all, as far as time goes, takes up half the polar year? And, moreover, it is precisely at this time that a decisive change takes place in the human mood, when the reality of the phenomenal world dissolves, when men slowly lose all sense of fixed points, of impulses from the external world.

Here, I am sure, lie the origins of "polar mentality", with all its apparent contradictions and enigmas. Here are the crossroads at which individuals with their variously composed personalities come to terms with the winter night.

Apart from scientists, who go to the Arctic for a specific purpose, all those who live alone and for whom the winter night is more or less a period of waiting suffer the same psychic demands.

My husband, who has always spent the winter alone, maintains that one gets used to viewing the world with the eyes of a hunter. When the moon is bright and the weather not too stormy one goes hunting, and at other times there is enough to do in running the hut, in cooking, baking, darning, and writing.

The extroverts among those who spend the winter here will always instinctively create for themselves a sphere of activity, and hence a sphere of reality that will save them when no impulse comes from without. Those who find their pleasure in meditation will withdraw into themselves, into regions of astonishing brightness; but those who are accustomed to yield to their inclination to idleness run the great danger of losing themselves in nothingness, of surrendering their senses to all the insane fantasies of overstretched nerves.

"Don't go for walks alone," says Karl. "It's a dangerous time. Seven weeks before Christmas the graves in Spitsbergen open."

This superstition suits the month of November, for in the entire polar night there is no time of the year so apt to mislead the waking mind and to conjure up fantastic images as now, when the last light is fading.

The date we mark today is 14 November. Yesterday Karl carried out his plan of going off to shoot more seals in Sense Bay where they are numerous. Although all the seals that turned up along our coast in the last few weeks were sighted by the hunters and fell victim to their marksmanship, which still never fails to astonish me, we need more fresh meat to add to our winter supplies.

I have washed the men's linen which, they asserted, would never be white again. And now I carry the clothes down to the freshwater spring to rinse them. With my skis on, a ski stick in one hand and the bucket of clothes in the other, it is a slow job to get along in the dark. But soon my eyes accustom themselves to the gloom, and I can clearly distinguish the lighter coast from the darker water. Slowly the mysterious twilight pictures rise again out of the mist. Everything is weighted under an enormous quilt; the snow deadens every soul.

I know the route of my daily walk perfectly, every stone and every rise in the ground, and still I am always being deceived. Suddenly a steep white wall rises in front of me; it seems to be quite close, but it is really a shallow rise some distance away. There a black hill juts out of the snow, a hill I have never noticed before, but then I see that it is only a small stone. There is a steep rise, but when I come to it my skis pass over level ground. Everything is distorted and dislocated in the swimming light, which affords the eye no fixed point by which to make judgments.

At last, after stumbling uncertainly around for three-quarters of an hour, constantly encountering new features that turn out not to be new after all, I reach the spring. I could not take a step further than the point at which my strength of will had set its goal—beyond is an infinite blackness in which everything is swallowed up.

The spring is still bubbling up strongly from beneath the snow, the water collects in hollowed-out stone troughs and then falls in tiny cascades down to the sea. The water is icy, and my hands become so stiff that I cannot wring out the last pieces of washing.

On the way back home the wind rises. The sea, now growing restless, beats against the frozen rocky shore. From the north a wind blows over the land, sweeping the dry snow up into columns, and then dies away, leaving everything again enveloped in quiet.

In the distance the dark outlines of the little hut emerge. Here, always on the same spot, I have for some time been startled by a remarkable fantasy. I imagine that something has risen out of the unquiet water in the last inlet before the hut, a dark form that is making its way toward me, bent, noiseless, and ineluctable. Again and again I try to banish this phantom, clear and sharp though its outlines may be in my imagination. How astonished I am then in the winter night, to find in an old case of books left behind by the hunter Nois an old number of *Allers Familienjournal*, containing an article on spectres, which reproduces a faithful likeness of my own phantom. There is the hobgoblin and the legendary sea serpent, and there also is the black figure as it rises out of the water and, stooping, slowly and inexorably approaches its victim. The caption reads: "A spectre of the shore which appears to fishermen." I did not want to go on reading then. I did not want to burden my imagination further with a more detailed description of the horrible fellow. When the light returns, once the long night is over, I will read it through to the end. For the time being it is enough to know that apparently this image rises wherever people live on lonely coasts.

With quickened steps I pass round the last inlet by the hut. Entering the little living room, the warmth and the friendly light of the little lamp burning so patiently in utter solitude makes me happy. There is an enticing smell from the coffee that I left on the stove and which I will drink when I have finished the day's washing.

But there is a second bucket of clothes to be rinsed. Now the wind is really rising, and the sea grows restless. The darkness of night is spreading, although it is only two in the afternoon. Of my two comrades there is nothing to be heard or seen. The distance and darkness seem to have swallowed them up.

None of us, I think, feels very well today on our solitary trips. Neither my husband, in the dark glacial valleys, nor Karl, lying in wait at Svendsen Bay on the shore of the dark sea for any *snadden*—the small seals—swimming past.

This time I notice, directly across my path, the tracks of a small animal. For weeks we have seen no trace of animals in Grey Hook, and this is worth striking a match for.

They are the prints of a ptarmigan. I can clearly recognise the marks of the three widespread toes of the only bird without webbed feet—apart from the snowy owl—that spends winter on the island. Apparently the bird, flying alone—as a rule they fly in coveys—came down on the edge of the coast looking for food. With a lighted match I follow its tracks until I reach a spot where marks in the snow reveal that it had scratched in vain for vegetation and then flown off again. Poor bird, this is not the right place for you. You will find nothing to support life on stony, dead Grey Hook.

Further to the south, in the fjord, a light blazes up. It might have been near or far. It was as bright as the flash from a gun, but as no shot followed I assume that it is Karl, returning from Svendsen Bay, who has probably lit his pipe.

Half an hour passes and nothing stirs. I use only two finger-tips to rinse the clothes and do not wring them out. At last, some distance away, Karl's figure passes noiselessly by.

We return home together. "What was it like in Svendsen Bay?" I ask.

"It's haunted," Karl replies. "You can't spend the night there."

We both laugh. We both know that ghosts are imaginary, but we both know also that imagination can become reality in the mind of a man who has lost all standard of reality in the loneliness and darkness.

When we enter the hut my husband is already there. He has prepared the dinner, that is to say, he has thawed out and warmed up the remains of yesterday's dinner of seal and lentils. After we have eaten, Karl, with an air of importance, draws from his pocket a crumpled newspaper. While in the hut at Svendsen Bay, Karl out of boredom had read the paper in which, in Tromsø, the lamp chimneys had been wrapped. These chimneys, which the *Lyngen* had brought up here, he had taken with him on his expedition. The newspaper, it is true, is pretty old, but for us it is still new.

"Now you shall hear the latest news from Svendsen Bay." He reads out a fairly long article about Spitsbergen. An able pen describes thundering glaciers and trumpeting whales; there is a story about a quite uncanny place, Bock Bay, a very close neighbour of Grey Hook. This bay has from earliest days been the home of the trolls—the earth spirits of the Norwegian sagas.

There is an account of those who are spending the winter there—Captain Ritter, whose wife has come from central Europe to find out about the *fortryllelse*—the bewitchments and enchantments—of the polar night. "This makes the lady the first European woman to spend the winter so far north."

This is, in any case, a great novelty for us, and the paper slowly makes the rounds. It is a long time since we have held a newspaper in our hands. Even the advertisement section on the back page is utterly fascinating:

Preserving sugar and vanilla pods from Per Bell,
     Garberggd.
Permanent waving at Johannesen, Tromsø.
Coffins, good, solid, cheap. Shrouds and wreaths also
     supplied. Hans Dahl, Storgt. 106.
Is your light out of order? Telephone 649 Sörrensen,
     Installasjonsforretning. Storgt. 110.

It is really touching, we think, how they manage to make themselves indispensable to each other, down below there in the world of men. How one man depends on others to earn his livelihood. That evening our conversation takes a philosophical turn. No, we don't have to look down on civilisation. We must not condemn it as a forced plant, as in our Spartan self-sufficient detachment from the world we would dearly like to. No, if only out of charity we must approve of decorated coffins, permanent waving, basins with running water, and burst pipes.

The growing darkness chains us to the hut. Each of us has made for himself a little sphere of work. My husband writes, studies, and reads. Karl always has something to mend, to solder, or to carve. He repairs watches and guns and mends our shoes. He carves knife handles out of walrus teeth, he sews *seltöffler*, attractive slippers made of seal skin. Karl knows something of every handicraft, and in addition he has the ability, peculiar to nearly all Norwegians, to tackle any situation with the most meagre equipment. He is what the Norwegians call for short an *altmüligman*—an everything-possible-man.

For myself, I will certainly have enough to do the whole winter night if I am to cope with the towering piles of mending that have accumulated during the years. It is laborious to have to sew everything by hand, particularly the long seams of the fur sleeping bags and waistcoats. Torn gloves and socks patiently await repair. Unfortunately I have forgotten how to turn a heel. The men make an effort to help me out with this. In desperation we unravel one sock after another in an attempt to fathom the mystery of the stitch. What makes it worse is that grandmothers in the north knit differently from Germans. There is great agitation. With beads of sweat on their brows and swearing horribly, holding the thin needles in their heavy hands, the men try with a kind of lunatic fervour to invent new knitting patterns for socks. My husband works according to a complicated system constructed on a geometrical formula, while Karl simply and happily knits long tubes pulled together at one end.

We take turns in running the house. This gives each of us in turn a full working day, and the menus undergo pleasing changes, since each of us has a quite different way of cooking. The men take on the meat days, for the meat is frozen as hard as stone and has first of all to be worked on with hatchet and hammer.

When it is my husband's turn to cook, oats play a big part. "Oats are wonderfully nourishing," he says and, no doubt, adds to himself that they are easy to prepare. Starting with breakfast, we have thick porridge in the English fashion, and at dinner—whatever the meat—oats go into the thick gravy. Even the bread, which has to be baked every day and prepared in the Spitsbergen hunter's fashion, and which is as light as biscuit, contains some oats. The hunters are always inventing new recipes, which they occasionally exchange with each other.

Karl is a master of the art of combination. On his cooking days we have ptarmigan mixed with seal, and sometimes ptarmigan, seal, and eider duck in one dish. Like a ship's cook, he knows how to stretch a meal "without anyone noticing anything"; he knows how to make mustard and can cut frozen seal meat so thin that it is good to eat and, spread on buttered toast and sprinkled with pepper and paprika, makes extremely tasty sandwiches. Karl makes "Turkish" coffee. All Norwegians detest any admixture in their coffee. The entire coffee ration for the day, ground very coarsely, is prepared at breakfast. Water is added to the thick brew remaining after we have had breakfast, and the pot is then left to bubble the whole day on the stoveplate. No Spitsbergen hunter ever starts any job until he has swallowed a few mouthfuls of hot coffee. Even the bear in front of the hut must wait for the moment of his death if the hunter has the opportunity to swallow a cup of coffee before shooting.

When it is my turn to cook, the men expect puddings and pastry. But on a ration of one egg a week it is not easy to produce the dumplings, pies, and pancakes that they order. Eider duck eggs, it is true, are twice as large as our chicken eggs, and are exquisitely coloured, pale green and black-speckled, but with the best will in the world it is impossible to beat the greasy egg white stiff.

When dinner has been eaten, when the bread is baking on the stoveplate and the temperature in the hut reaches the top—plus forty degrees—while the ground temperature is always below zero, it is advisable to seek the horizontal position. During these hours of rest on our bunks we tell each other stories. The hunters have a rich experience to draw on. They talk about their trips in the waters of Spitsbergen, Greenland, and the White Sea. Karl has been through two shipwrecks in northeast Spitsbergen; he and his comrades had to make their way across the pack ice until they were picked up, on the first occasion by a sealer, and on the second by hunters on Verlegen

Hook. He tells us about one of his *smafangst* trips—summer seal hunting in an open boat—when the boat in which he and his companions were journeying was caught fast in the ice of the Hinlopen Strait. Since they were not equipped for a winter's stay, the three of them, with only one sleeping bag between them, and galoshes on their feet, went on foot over the ice of New Friesland to Wijde Bay and from there to Dickson Bay whence Oxaas, the same hunter who had once looked after Karl and his shipwrecked companions on Verlegen Hook, rowed them across to Advent Anchorage.

In contrast to these involuntary wanderings of Karl, my husband tells us of his more or less voluntary trips and cross-country expeditions at different seasons of the year. From his winter quarters at Kings Bay he crossed the Holtedahl plateau to Wood Bay; once he crossed the seven glaciers to Magdalena Bay, and another time Ice Fjord. He tells us of his frequent trips to the post in early spring, either alone or by dog sleigh, from the north coast, through Wijde Bay, and over the glacier to Sassen Bay and to the radio station at the Norwegian coal mine at Longyear Valley. He also tells us of his expeditions, when quite a young chap, with the Prince of Monaco, crossing from Bell Sound to the Stor Fjord.

The two hunters exchange reminiscences, detail their observations, and discuss other hunters, and on their maps they mark out the best routes across glaciers, seas, and fjords.

In the evening hours, which incidentally have long ceased to coincide with the evening hours of our latitude in the lands of the sun, we play patience. The Spitsbergen hunter's favourite game of patience is called "the wicked lady". It is brain-rackingly complicated and hardly ever comes out. Nonetheless it is on the outcome of this game of patience that the ever-recurring serious, fateful questions are hung: "How many foxes, how many bears will the hunt bring in? Will the pack ice come, or won't it?"

Meanwhile the world out-of-doors falls into deepest night. The mountains are no more than white shadows, the sea no more than a black shadow—until that too dissolves away. And then everything is dead.

In this pitch darkness we cannot move far from the hut. I make the smallest possible turns around the hut—all that is left of my walks. When it is not snowing we spend hours outside the hut chopping and sawing wood by the light of the hurricane lamp. Sometimes drizzling rain descends on us out of the high darkness, sometimes a drizzle of snow.

The wind that, rising and falling, lasts for days is in fact our last link with the reality of the world, and at night, when it has grown quiet in the hut, it dominates our consciousness. We know the storm now by its speech. We know all its signs. We know from what direction it is coming to us, and does come, even when we cannot see a weathervane.

Winds from the west begin with the rumbling blows of the surf on the cliffs by the water. The sound of these storms is ringing, roaring, sonorous, and heavy.

Winds from the north rise to an unbroken thunder.

Winds from the east are brisk and lively. Although everything around the hut has long been buried deep under snow, these storms still find something to shake and rattle vehemently.

But the wind from the south is mournful and gentle. There is a humming in the distance. Far below, at the southern end of the fjord, it falls down the mountains and passes over the hut, remarkably gentle and mild. Never are we so conscious of our solitude as when the south wind blows, singing through the distant valleys.

10

The Bewitching Polar Night

In mid-December the mists clear.

Whoever has looked at the moon through a telescope knows the emotional impact that the bright cold petrifaction and silence of that strange heavenly body makes on men. We were moved in the same way, when after weeks of stumbling round in unending darkness, we found ourselves translated into a world that, familiar and yet completely new, surrounded us with its radiance.

It is as though we are on another planet, somewhere else in universal space, where in nameless peace bright mountains rest and the light speaks with a mute eloquence.

Is this really our Grey Hook? The bright frozen land lies motionless in the clear air. Every wrinkle and fold of the mountain, every rise and fall of the land, is radiantly visible. Land and cliff, joined into one tremendously animated structure, rise dazzling white out of a black sea into the dusky night sky.

We go out into the bright land. In the valleys the wind howls, over the plain the snow is driven like a glistening river, but calm and unmoved the mountains soar into the star-glittering heavens.

Bright veils detach themselves from the sky. As though stirred by the gentlest breath of wind they float in ever brighter and broader waves across the whole heaven. We watch the shining rhythm of the spheres until the veils disappear, and come to ourselves, small beings struggling forward mute and heavy through the storm on the earth.

We climb the steep snow slopes. The fox traps are all yawning open, the driven snow raging through them. From the crest of the hill we can see the many gleaming frozen mountains of Spitsbergen soaring upward. Whatever we feel, it is not loneliness as we stare into the distance. It is as though we are enclosed in a miraculous world.

Rushing downhill and across the plain, the wind at our backs, we return to our hut by the sea. The effortless journey through the glittering moon-shiny land is wonderful, intoxicating. But strangely, once back in our hut under the snow, we are again content. The little room rests like a beneficent shadow on our spirits, which are thoroughly excited by all the intoxicating brightness.

But the men are seized by wanderlust. The next day, when I go for my walk, making large circles round our chimney, I can hear them chattering away in the hut under the snow. They are tidying up and talking, and grinding large quantities of coffee at an unusual hour. Then I know what's up.

"We'll only be away a few days," they say as they separate, one going inland by the fjord, the other eastward. "We must keep an eye on the traps. Sometimes in winter the live foxes eat the dead ones in the traps."

To get over the feeling of loneliness I throw myself, as usual, into hard work. I polish and wash, and have to crawl out to the snow hole countless times to fill the snow bucket and crawl back as many times to empty it. But I am glad to get out of the dark hut onto the mute and mighty ice stage on which the magnificent play of the polar night is enacted.

Northern lights of incredible intensity stream over the sky; their bright rays, shooting downward, look like gleaming rods of glass. They break out from a tremendous height and seem to be falling directly toward me, growing brighter and clearer, in radiant lilacs, greens, and pinks, swinging and whirling around their own axis in a wild dance that sweeps over the entire sky, and then, in drifting undulating veils, they fade and vanish.

It is only the laundry woman in me that stands alone in the hut washing clothes. All my other senses are out-of-doors in the bewildering magic light, the indescribable enchantment of the Arctic night. The clothes, which I hang up at once, freeze stiff as boards, and my hands turn to ice. But the hunters say that clothes bleach well in moonlight. Obediently I take my "walk" every day. I buckle on my skis and take turns round the hut, ten times round by the left, ten times by the right. I don't risk going any further out.

The snow that blankets Grey Hook is undisturbed; far and wide there is no trace of an animal. The foxes creep into the mountains looking for ptarmigan, and the ptarmigan live under the snow. The few reindeer herds that are still to be found on the island are grazing inland down the fjord, in quiet distant valleys never touched by human feet. The night is glorious, the black mountains seem now to be chiselled out of white marble, like all the fantastic peaks along the broad sweeping coasts of the fjord. In the south the tremendous rocky throne of Bock Bay, in the southwest the flat triangle of Cape Roos, and further to the west the jagged summits of Liefde Bay. The sea is a deep black-blue. The small black silver-edged waves beat gently on the shore. I can hear the noise made by the pebbles as they are carried along in the ebb and flow of the waves. Northern lights drift silently across the sky.

The Eskimos have given a beautiful interpretation of the mysterious undulation of the light. They believe that they can see the spirits of their departed in its drifting veils. This serene light has in it something that yearns toward the earth, something sheltering, consoling, promising, and yet utterly mute in its remoteness.

If people at home knew how wonderful it is here. It is a pity that in Europe they can imagine only the terrors of the polar night. It is true that in the encyclopedias they can read about the wonders of the polar world, but they have no idea that under this radiant heaven a man's spirit is also calm, clear, and radiant.

Now there is no longer even a glimmer of day, not even at noon. Around the whole horizon only deep starry night. Day and night, throughout its circular course, the moon is in the sky, the pole star almost at the zenith, and around it, every twenty-four hours, the entire starry firmament revolves.

There is a howling wind again today, sweeping over the plain, but the mountains of Grey Hook are moon-like in their clarity. Moon-like without an atmosphere, moon-like in their dead immobility.

Slowly the wind covers the traces of the men's skis, which have lasted for many days, one pair going east and one south, visible for a long way in the moonlight. Out on the plain the wind whirls the snow into straight and uncannily high columns. In the bright moonlight they look like white figures moving erect and solemn toward the coast. At the steep bank they pause for a moment, seem to bend slowly at the knee and, stooping slightly forward, to descend the high cliffs and, like white shadows, to disperse over the black sea.

Bewildering beyond anything is the wild howling of the wind against the unmoving gleaming face of the frozen earth, and the musically gentle dance of the northern lights in the sky. I try to find similes to convey the bewildering strangeness of this experience. I think the contrasts in perception make the same impact on our feelings as would, for example, the playing of a noisy Berlioz symphony in a theatre where the stage is set in a scene of classic calm. Or as if we saw a serenely smiling man commit murder, murder everything that comes within range of his smile. The polar night displays the world in a clash of rhythms that make us central Europeans dizzy.

For a painter, too, the accustomed attitude to landscape no longer fits his experience. Landscape and northern lights can scarcely be brought together in a picture. Light and landscape remain two separate things. If he responds to the spirit of the landscape, the light is alien and its dimensions exaggerated. If he loses himself in the light, then the heaven becomes the shining living picture, and the earth is dead and expressionless.

Today I cannot rid myself of the impression made by a vivid dream. In it something commanded me to repair the stove with a mixture of fire-clay and beach pebbles; this would stop it from smoking.

I get the ice axe down from the roof and go out hunting for beach pebbles. They are not so easy to find. Everything is yards deep under snow, and frozen hard. Nor can I get any on the beach itself, for it is high tide and the water is lapping against the high snowdrifts of the bay as though in a gigantic china basin. But in front of the woodpile where the wind and the driving snow are deflected I find, about five feet down, some stones that have been washed smooth. I dig at them and the sparks fly, but not a single stone is loosened. The ground is frozen hard as steel, and for the first time I understand why the dead cannot be buried in Spitsbergen in wintertime, and why the hunters, to save them from the bears and foxes, keep their dead comrades with them in the hut right through the winter.

Back in the hut I crush three bricks into powder and another into small pieces and, since there is no clay, mix them together with paste and spread the mixture over the inside of the stove. There are enormous holes eaten out by rust, and large cracks; it is a miracle that it has been burning at all. But later, when I light the fire, it smokes worse than ever. While I was trying to repair it I noticed that it was sinking toward the centre; the rings of the stoveplate no longer fit, and now it is completely useless.

Frozen stiff with cold, and quite desperate, I crawl into my bunk.

During the night Karl returns. What will he do without a fire? I can hear him busying himself about the stove, cursing softly, and then there is an infernal crash followed by a loud rumbling noise. Then I can hear Karl creeping out of the hut and back again at least twenty times. Behind the hut he shovels snow and inside the hut I can hear him hammering. At last I can hear a fire crackling away. Then a knocking on my door.

"Are you still alive? Come out quick. I've got a wonderful surprise for you."

When I come into the living room it is free of smoke for the first time since we have been on the island. Instead of the catastrophic stove there is a tiny baby stove that had been brought along to replace the stove in one of the refuge huts. It is so small that Karl has had to stand it on a case to raise it to a manageable height, and now it is glowing and giving out a fantastic amount of heat.

"The old stove fell to pieces," Karl says apologetically. Now I know that my dream has come true, though in a roundabout way.

Today, behind the mountains of Grey Hook, a gigantic glowing arc rose, a white fire in the sombre night sky. Then at its centre the moon appeared. The magnificent arc was still rising behind the mountains when it closed in an enormous circle this side of the mountains, becoming more superbly impressive, infinitely miraculous. Against that tremendous burning circle of light the earthly scene is dead and shadowy, an extinct orb.

The moon ring, Karl says, means bad weather.

In the night after its appearance the storm breaks with explosive force. Something or other falls from the roof—I think it is the oars—and the heavy ice anchor rolls to and fro. From my small window I can watch the furious tumult of the snow, cloudy masses lit up by the moon, driving in wild serpentine movements over the ice-covered earth.

I wonder whether Hermann is on his way. Could anyone keep going in such a blizzard? Would he not be hurled along the ground like a piece of wood? Shall I ask Karl whether there is any way of going to the help of a man caught in a storm like this?

Karl is fast asleep in his drawer bunk under the quivering roof. He does not seem to hear the storm. I don't want to awaken him. He would only say what I have already been saying to myself: anybody who ventures out in this is lost.

The thundering of the storm and the sea is frenzied. And now it grows pitch dark. The black inferno rages the whole night through. All the dangers of the Wijde Bay hunting grounds rise before me. The storm through which perhaps a solitary man is fighting his way is terribly frightening.

Toward morning the storm dies away as suddenly as it broke. Karl shovels the snow from the door. Again Grey Hook is lying in clear moonlight, in peaceful night, under the remote tremulous lights.

Our hut is now completely buried under snow. The furrows cut by last night's storm, frozen hard, strike clear across the roof as though there were no hut there at all. Restless and anxious I pace up and down outside the hut. The day seems endless. At last, toward evening, Hermann comes home, covered with hoarfrost, smiling, and hung with foxes.

"Where were you when the storm broke last night?" Karl and I ask at the same moment.

"Between the Russian hut and the Villa Rave. But I managed very well." No more words are wasted on the storm. The hunters keep things like that to themselves. And that is perhaps what is most splendid in the life of these hunters, this close juxtaposition of life and death, this reticence about their greatest experiences.

It is full moon. No central European can have any idea of what this means on the smooth frozen surface of the earth. It is as though we were dissolving in moonlight, as though the moonlight were eating us up. It makes no difference when we go back into the hut under the snow after a moonlight trip. The light seems to follow us everywhere. One's entire consciousness is penetrated by the brightness; it is as though we were being drawn into the moon itself.

We have been out in the moonlight a great deal, for some pack ice has entered the fjord. A whole iceberg is stranded on the shore in front of our hut. Moving gently with the current and gleaming in the moonlight, the ice floes, piled high with freshly fallen snow, float by our hut. We stand spellbound and stare. Again and again we climb the moon-shiny mountains to keep watch over the sea. It does not look as though all the pack ice is coming our way.

We cannot escape the brightness. I take it particularly badly, and the hunters maintain that I am moonstruck. What I would like best of all is to stand all day on the shore, where in the water the rocking ice floes catch and break the light and throw it back at the moon. But the men are very strict with me. They do not let me out of their sight and often keep me under house arrest. And then I lie down in my little room, where the moonlight filters green through the small snowed-up window. Neither the walls of the hut nor the roof of snow can dispel my fancy that I am myself moonlight, gliding along the glittering spines and ridges of the mountains, through the white valleys…

"Now Chrissie has got *rar*," says Karl, shaking his head. "*Ishavet kaller*. You must be reasonable." *Rar* is a strangeness that overcomes many who spend the winter in polar regions. *Ishavet kaller*, or "the Arctic calls", is what the Spitsbergen hunters say when one of their comrades, for mysterious reasons, throws himself into the sea.

And as though food were the cure for all ills, Karl gives me enormous helpings of seal meat when it is his turn to cook; it is dripping with the cod liver oil he has poured over it. He breaks all our strict meat-rationing rules and speaks to me persuasively. "Do eat. You're too thin for the winter night. It would be quite stupid to save meat now. Soon we'll get the pack ice, with plenty of bear meat, and when the fjord freezes over, the eider ducks will come to our coast. Last year on Bangen Hook a seal came on land in February, and we shot it. Soon we'll have heaps of meat."

To please me, Karl has, without telling me, taken my sewing basket and brought masculine order into the tangled confusion of wools and threads. All the different wools are now wound neatly on small, prettily carved wooden boards, and the buttons, which during my collecting mania in the autumn I cut from the clothes washed ashore, are tidied away in a carved box.

I have lost all desire to do housework, and the men bake heart-shaped waffles and all kinds of cake. They put sugar and raisins and other dried fruit in the ordinary bread, for Christmas will soon be on us. All the hunters in Spitsbergen are baking now, even those who have lived alone for years. Our neighbour, old Sven Ohlson, in Biscay Hook, is said to bake so much that even in the spring he can still entertain his guests with frozen cakes. Arctic ships, seeking shelter from the storm, often come to his part of the coast. And when no ships come, Sven still bakes for his imaginary guests, pickles reindeer tongues, and preserves the best parts of his bears.

We have a charming Christmas Eve. It is true that toward the end of our preparations we have reached an explosive pitch of nervousness. All three of us are helping to cook the Christmas dinner, all three of us need water for washing, and the stoveplate is no bigger than four square inches. All of us bustle around in the little living room preparing our surprises. Nobody wants to go into the little passage room, where the thermometer shows thirty degrees of frost. Out-of-doors the storm is raging with its accustomed ferocity. We have never been so much in each other's way, and the whole day, to save space, we take it in turns to lie down in the bunk. We have to exercise the greatest self-control to keep the peace.

But when in the evening we light the candles on the little tree that Karl has carved, a stem with three cross beams, we are overcome by a deep solemnity. The little table on which our presents are laid out is astonishingly full. There are salad servers, which Karl has carved for me out of the mahogany table leg washed ashore. They have a really gothic look about them, the scooping spoon and the stabbing fork. There is a whole row of Norwegian books, taken from a hunter's chest, easy for me to read, the titles freshly painted on the spines in my husband's delicate script.

The present that Hermann and I give to Karl is a series of drawings illustrating his life next winter. He had wanted a Lapp girl as his companion, and here she is, trapping foxes and bears, and making coffee for Karl all day long, while Karl spends his time taking care of the triplets with which she has presented him.

Our Christmas dinner is elegant. Each of us has prepared one course. We have ptarmigan with rice and stewed apricots and, to crown it all, a caramel cream made of eider duck eggs, burnt sugar, and condensed milk. The cream tastes horribly of seaweed and mud. I cannot swallow a single spoonful, but the men are ready to lick their plates. Karl says it is a devilishly fine dish such as you could get only at the Ritz Hotel in Tromsø, and the two of them regret that they did not choose the South Cape of Spitsbergen for their winter quarters because there the birds often lay their eggs at the end of May, whereas up here in the north they rarely ever find an ice-free place for laying before the end of June. And now that we have squandered our last egg for Christmas, they will have to wait six months before I can make another caramel cream for them.

New Year's Eve we celebrate with raspberry juice and surgical spirit. Incidentally, that was the only occasion during the entire winter that we made use of our medical stores. (When Karl had a toothache, which happened frequently, he cured it according to an old hunter's prescription by drinking a cupful of spirits and water.) The unaccustomed alcohol puts us in high spirits, and we tell our fortunes in the old Norwegian and old German way. We melt some leaden shot, and on the stroke of twelve, outside the hut, Karl fires off a shot into the dark winter night. The hunter Björnes does that every year too, although he always spends the winter alone, the only man in the whole length of Wijde Bay.

11

The Unending Darkness

Now everything around us is quite dead; even the battering
of the storm has ceased. A heavy mist weighs on everything; the hut is shrouded in stillness and darkness. It seems
to me as if only now has the real night fallen, and slowly my
courage begins to seep away. Perhaps the sun will never come
back again. Perhaps it is dark all over the world.

My husband calms my fears. Again and again, on little
scraps of paper, he marks the course of the sun, which since
23 December has been on its way back to us. He calculates
the degrees and minutes for me, demonstrating that the sun
is now as near to us as it was distant on 9 December. But I
am in despair. All his explanations tell me only how far away
the sun is. There is no glimmer of light to show that it is
coming nearer, and although seventy-eight days of darkness
have already passed, there are still another fifty-four days before,
for the first time, the sun will peep for a few seconds over the
southern horizon.

With iron consistency, as though my life depended on it, I
take my walk every day. It is scarcely a walk any more, rather a

daily crawl on all fours close to the walls of the hut. Round and round mechanically, in circles, ten times, twenty times, over the uneven snowdrifts that have frozen hard as steel. I know every inch of it and go with my eyes closed. At first I was uncertain in the darkness. Often I would suddenly imagine a bear in front of me, but now I have found a way of dealing with my fear. At regular intervals I beat on the walls of the hut with my fist, so that the noise will scare away anything that may be in the neighbourhood.

The days pass uneventfully, without any real work, without a consoling glimpse into the reality of the world. At night we lie down, neither tired nor wakeful, encompassed by the unending darkness and the profound quiet.

Surrounded by this boundless deadness and rigidity of everything physical, one's living senses begin slowly to go their own way. More frequently and more brightly as the winter is prolonged, a strange light spreads before the inner eye, a remote and yet familiar vision. It is as though here, in this apartness, we develop a particularly sharp awareness of the mighty laws of the spirit, of the unfathomable gulf between human magnitudes and eternal truth. Outside of time, everything is annihilated. The imprisoned senses circle in the past, in a scene without spatial dimensions, a play in which time stands still.

Often I see the flowers and trees of the distant sun world, but I do not see them as I used to see them. They are glowing with colour and piercingly beautiful. Their most secret meaning lives in their growth and their colour. But the people who live under the sun seem distant and small to me. With bent heads they are running round in circles, the circles of their anxieties and troubles. Only a few of them see the glory of the sun.

Early morning—is it a relief or a disturbance?—the sound of the little coffee mill breaks through the multicoloured scenes of another world. It is with difficulty that my mind comes back to the reality; slowly I realise that another pitch-black day has broken in the hut under the snow.

We sit silently at our breakfast and warm our icy hands round the coffee cups. We can see our breath in the lamplight, and each of us notices silently how pale and careworn the others look.

"Perhaps we haven't been normal for a long time," Karl says suddenly. "We can't judge ourselves, we're so used to each other. Somebody from Europe, somebody on whom the sun shines regularly, he could perhaps tell us. But it isn't likely that someone like that will come this way."

"No, it will be a long time before anyone comes," we say, and look through the window at the white walls of driven snow. From an upper corner of the window frame, where the heat inside the room has melted some of the snow, the black night looks in. All the edges of the room are white, and the nails in the walls are covered with hoarfrost. Otherwise the hut is completely black from soot and smoke. I do not need to scrub the floor; the room would never dry out, the men say, and we would then merely be sitting on ice. So there is nothing for me to do except observe with

a painter's eye the curious contrasts between the black of the hut and the whiteness of anything that we bring in from outside.

The foxes are now fantastically white, and the ptarmigan unspotted; the blocks of snow that we bring in for melting look dazzlingly bright in the dark corner by the stove.

Up here one must be broadminded enough not to be pedantic. I see life too with other eyes. Forgotten are all externals; here everything is concerned with simple being. The hut is a covered hollow, without which we would freeze; the primitive food must be eaten, for it keeps us alive. And we can even play with sooty cards, although hearts and diamonds are as black as spades. They help us to pass the time of darkness, and that is their value.

At the beginning of December the men had said that by Christmas the dark days would be past. Now I no longer believe them, for it is January and the blackness and fearfulness of the winter night seem only now really to have begun. I do not know how many days it is that the howling and whistling of the wind, piercingly shrill and unbroken, has been going on and the hard pellets of hail have been whipping our roof, faster and faster and without a pause. I have lost count of the number of days since we went out and of the hours the men spend each day shovelling snow to keep the door of the hut more or less free. And if anyone ventures a step out of doors into the raging night to read the instruments, he comes back after a few seconds breathless, eyebrows, eyelashes, and clothes rimed with frost. When the door is opened, whirling snow comes into the hut; the icy air rushes like a cloud into the room and makes straight for the bunks. The dampness collects under the bunks and both of them are as dripping wet as landing stages. The walls around the bunks have an inch-thick coating of ice. I no longer even try to dry out the fur coverlets of the bunks over the stove, or to thaw out the ice on the walls with the paraffin lamp; it is quite hopeless, and the two men take everything as it comes.

Today Karl is washing a dirty seal skin that he had removed from a barrel in the snow when there was still moonlight. He washes it with soap and soda in boiling water and then nails the dripping skin, reeking of oil, onto the roof of the hut. He wants to make gloves of it when it is dry, "for the winter".

"I thought winter's been here a long time already," I interject.

"Winter in Svalbard begins in February," the two of them say as one man. "It starts when the temperatures of minus forty and minus fifty set in, and the sea and the fjords begin to freeze over." And I had thought that once the light returns all difficulties would be overcome.

Although it is not yet noon, Karl has already stopped work. Nobody, he thinks, should overdo work during the winter night; it is unhealthy. So he lies down again on his bunk and starts singing. He has a beautiful voice, but his repertoire has shrunk remarkably during the days of darkness. His jolly mountaineering songs are forgotten. He no longer sings the song of the master butcher Jule, who slaughters through four verses and in the chorus squeals and grunts like a pig. He no longer sings about the "people without fingers who play the piano, and those without noses who sneeze". He sings but one sad song, the song of an unhappy infatuated gypsy, which he has probably picked up from a gramophone record. He sings it whatever he is doing—washing, cooking, getting ready for sleep—and it sounds particularly doleful when his funereal voice emerges from the depths of his sleeping bag, slow as a funeral march. The mournful song from the Hungarian plain would sound sad if Karl, with his imperturbable Norwegian good humour, did not himself begin to make fun of his own melancholy.

Each of us has developed his own little eccentricity, which is growing more marked; this is said to happen to practically all people who spend the winter here. I seem to have a passion for sewing, mending, and polishing. Hermann nourishes a lunatic miserliness about everything made of wood. Every stick of wood that is added to the fire he follows with the eyes of a hawk, and he has hidden all the matches and pencils under the mattress of his bunk, on which he sits like a Cerberus, mounting guard. Karl, when he is not singing, has a talking mania. He talks and talks, incredibly quickly, making me think of a little steam engine about to explode. What is so odd is that he himself no longer seems to notice that he is telling a story for the sixth or seventh time. And again and again he puts the big question: "Where shall we spend the winter next year?" He has thought of a number of good places. White Island right to the east, which is perpetually frozen over, and where walruses are to be found in their hundreds in the spring. Or should we rent a hut in Flat Hook? There's a river there with salmon, and we can fish right through the winter night. Or shall we go to Bock Bay, with its volcanic springs? We could run hot water directly into the hut, and the lady could have baths all the time.

And when we remind him that he had wanted to attend the seamen's school in Tromsø in the coming year and it is about time he began studying here and now, for he has his textbooks in the bunk, he only sighs and says it would be nonsense for him to take the mariner's examination, for he cannot tear himself away from Spitsbergen.

Today we are having our last but one meal of seal meat. After that we still have four ptarmigan. The Lofoten fishermen's dish that Karl has introduced, potatoes roasted in cod liver oil, is rationed. And the foxes are to be skinned only one by one. Their meat is now our iron ration and has to last us till the spring. We urgently need some bears to keep up our fresh-meat vitamin supply.

Karl is always consulting the cards. "Will the pack ice come, or won't it? Shall we have bears?" Gradually all our thoughts revolve around the pack ice. Strangely enough, my fear of the pack ice has vanished. I am beginning to think in exactly the same terms as the hunters. I, too, long for the pack ice, for the mysterious whiteness out there in the blackness, which brings precious gifts to the hunters cut off from the world in the winter night—bears, fresh meat, furs, excitement, incident, the chase, and… more foxes. Foxes that live on the drift ice, foxes that spend their lives creeping after the bears and eating whatever they leave behind uneaten from their meals. Foxes, and that is the salient point, that make straight for the traps when they reach land because they have never seen one before and are innocent of distrust.

But the pack ice is a chancy thing. "It's out there, a dozen miles or so from the coast," Hermann says. But the powerful current from the west keeps it from coming in closer; a violent and protracted storm from the northwest or the northeast might bring it in. And the wind is of course incalculable. Sometimes the ice reaches the north coast in autumn, sometimes only in the spring. Sometimes it comes and immediately drifts away again, sometimes it stays the whole summer through, and some years it never comes at all.

The patience of the hunters is remarkable. Often they come up here from Norway, fishermen and sailors, use all their savings to equip their little expeditions, get themselves put ashore from a ship, and then wait, wait for the ice that is to bring the bears. Bear hunting in Spitsbergen needs patience. It's a question of luck. The hunting of the bear itself is perhaps not the most difficult thing; it is being able to wait in solitude and darkness.

"How can you tell in the darkness when the pack ice is coming?" I ask the men.

"By the noise, my dear creature; by the cold, by the steady low temperature."

"I can smell the pack ice from afar," Karl says enthusiastically. "The first thing the bears do when they come to a hut is to smash the chimney."

"How awful! And why the chimney particularly?"

"Heaven knows. But they always do. Perhaps just in playfulness. Or perhaps they are disturbed by the sight of it, as they never see a stovepipe on their pack ice. They break all the windowpanes too, unless they are protected by shutters. They don't know what glass is, and they break through it, perhaps just out of curiosity."

There was a bear that broke the window of Björnes' hut and put his paws right into the box of margarine that was on the table under the window. That was a pleasant surprise for Björnes, who was sitting at the table.

The seventy-year-old man who had spent the previous winter with Karl was alone in the hut while Karl was out on one of his expeditions. A bear came up to the hut and pushed the stovepipe down through the roof. When Karl returned, the old man was sitting by the wrecked stove, covered in smoke and dust, and ice cold, his face beaming as he told that the first bear had arrived.

One story succeeds another. Karl has shot twenty-seven bears, as many as he has years, and all of them in summer when he and his companions were at sea hunting seal and walrus. "You have to lie absolutely still on the ice and try to look like a seal when a bear approaches. You have to let him come quite near, but not nearer than ten yards because at that distance a bear can hurl himself on his victim like a huge cat."

My husband tells us of the bears he has seen in summer. They obviously enjoy the warmth of the sun; they sit in the sun and rub their bellies with pleasure. Once he encountered a bear during the winter night as he was creeping on all fours along a narrow icy strip of rock by the shore, under the overhanging snowdrifts. The frightened bear suddenly rose before him, growling, but was immediately set on by Hermann's dog with such violence that it jumped into the water and swam off. Then there was the bear that spent the entire summer on Prince Charles Foreland. A Norwegian hunter and his newly wed wife, who put ashore on the island to spend the winter there, came upon the bear one day, shot him, and banqueted on him for many weeks.

Bears are wonderful divers. When they have spied a seal on the edge of the ice, they swim underwater and come up exactly on the spot where the seal is and so cut him off from the water. Female bears drop their young at the end of February and beginning of March. At this time they go ashore and dig out caves in the snow for themselves and their progeny. Spitsbergen hunters say they have often come across these caves, which are dug in the shape of a capital T or of a loop, and slope upward from the entrance to keep the warmth in. The young bears remain with their mothers for two years, until they can look after themselves. That is why female bears are often found with cubs of different ages. If anything happens to the mother, another female bear or a male bear takes over the care of the young.

Female bears are very strict mothers. Karl once watched one of them who was about to creep unobserved up to a seal. The young ones wanted to accompany her, but she beat them so severely that the little ones were sent bouncing across the ice like balls. Another hunter saw a female bear in the water box her cub's ears soundly because it did not want to take to the water alone.

Some of their stories are about incidents for which the hunters themselves were responsible. One of them went out to inspect his spring-gun bear trap. He was surprised to see two bears lying in front of it; he could not imagine how two bears could have been killed by one shot. As he drew near, the female bear, which had lain down by its dead cub, rose up and attacked him. Thoughtlessly, he had gone out without his gun, and to reach his hut in safety he had to discard one piece of clothing after the other and throw it behind him. Each time the bear stopped and sniffed at the garment inquisitively, and the hunter gained time and got away. Another hunter took home the young cubs of a mother bear he had shot and raised them in his hut. As they grew older they went out on their own for walks on the ice. One day they rushed back yelping, followed by a large bear. The cubs had never seen a large bear and sought safety with their human foster father.

6 January. At dinner today we eat our last seal meat. It is not at all good; it tastes like fish stewed in aluminium. The potatoes taste like chestnuts burnt to a cinder and the sauerkraut like *papier-mâché*. But our appetites are still big, and we eat impressive quantities. Karl is quite fat from eating, although he is very pale and his eyes are growing more and more colourless. But that is what happens in the winter night.

Another discovery causes us extreme annoyance. There must have been a mistake in the provisions delivered to us, and instead of the dark rye meal we have a sack of wheat flour. We had counted on the vitamins in the coarsely ground rye meal.

All our provisions are completely frozen. The eggs drop like stones out of their shells and the condensed milk rattles in its tins. The carrots and celery sticks, which up to now I have carried from one place to another, like a cat with its young, to keep them in a more favourable temperature, are also frozen hard.

It is becoming more and more urgent to get fresh meat.

The wind has no idea of blowing consistently from the northeast, to bring the pack ice—it changes direction as often as three times a day, and the temperature fluctuates between minus thirty degrees and minus two within twelve hours.

Today, 9 January, the weather clears and for the first time we see, about midday, a small, weak, reddish light on the southern horizon. We are quite wild with joy.

Even if the world has gone up in flames, the sun is still here, and the earth is moving in its appointed course.

This is followed again by days of the blackest night.

Today, 22 January, there is for the first time colour in the sky. In the south a lemon-yellow glimmer fading into a transparent blue. But over our heads all the stars are still winking. For the first time we can see ourselves by the light of day and we are quite horrified. We look pale yellow, like plants kept in a cellar, and our skin is flaccid and shrivelled.

25 January. It is so light today that things have again taken visible shape in our sight. The mountains of Grey Hook are before us in all their palpable mass. The incorporeal wavering and dancing of every outline in the uncertain light is over. It is as though we are standing again for the first time firmly on our feet on the familiar earth. The men go into the mountains to look for ptarmigan. They have a craving for fresh blood, they say. They come back tired and depressed. There is no trace of a living thing far and wide.

On the 26 January the wind at last begins to blow strongly from the north. Twenty-five degrees below zero. The sky is overcast. Everything is shrouded in thickly falling snow. Karl dashes into the hut. A flock of eider ducks is swimming along past the shore. The two men rush out with their guns. Too late! The whole column of fifty to sixty birds is swimming out to sea. But it is still possible that the birds will remain near the coast for the next few days, and we decide to dig the boat out of the snow. At the moment only its ice-covered rowlocks are showing above ground.

The boat has frozen into a single lump of ice. The three of us set to work with axe and shovel. It is not so easy to chisel the seats out of the ice, but after two hours' work we get the boat free at last.

On the 27 January a snowstorm rages from the east. The eider ducks again come in close to the shore. Sheltered from the wind they flutter to and fro, keeping a part of the water open. The rest of the bay is entirely covered with ice slime, like a sticky grey paste blowing out to sea in the raging east wind. The hunters have shot two birds from land. The birds are lying between the coast and the stranded iceberg around which the ice slime is drifting. Watching from the hut I see the men, half-hidden by the whirling snow, push the boat into the water. They row carefully in the narrow channel of water sheltered from the wind by the frozen cliffs. It is very hazardous to take the boat out today; it would not be the first time that a boat caught in the ice slime had been driven helplessly out to sea.

Between the gusts of snow I can see the boat. It seems to have got into the slime. The sticky masses of ice seem to have closed in on the oars. I can see the men rowing with all their might for the shore, but the boat does not move from the spot. They keep it in violent motion to prevent it from freezing fast. A few dreadful minutes pass, and then the distance between them and the shore lessens.

With the last of their strength they pull the boat up. Defeated and smiling they come back to the hut. They had risked their lives for vitamins. The little dead birds, which they could not reach, drift out to sea with the ice slime.

1 February: beginning of winter.

The snowdrifts in front of the hut are growing into mountains. The men shovel without a break. They ponder the advisability of cutting a hole in the roof, to ensure a way out into the open for the future.

"Will the pack ice come? Will it not come?" Untiringly Karl consults the cards.

12

The Pack Ice and the First Bear

The wind remains strong and toward evening veers to the north. The temperature falls to thirty-five below. The next day the wind is still raging from the northeast. Now the pack ice must come. In the evening the temperature falls to forty below, and Karl can smell the pack ice in the air.

In a sort of delirium he lays out the cards, while outside in the darkness the storm howls. "How many bears will come to our coast? How many bears will Mrs. shoot if she is alone in the hut?"

"One bear for Mrs." announce the cards. Karl hurriedly gives me a lesson. "When you've shot a bear, you must skin it at once while it is still warm. But you mustn't eat the liver. It's poisonous. You must remove the gall bladder carefully, and keep it in spirit. The chemists in Tromsø pay eight kroner, eight kroner if you bring them a bear's gall bladder in spirit. It's good for rheumatism, cures toothache, and every kind of boil."

"Bear gall is supposed to contain radium," my husband interjects. "When we were on polar ships we had nearly always drunk the spirit before we reached Tromsø."

The storm continues all night. I am awakened early by the noise of the men rushing to and fro, slamming doors, and calling to each other out in the open. Then the door of my little room bursts open and my husband calls in. "The ice is right here. The ice is here."

For sheer joy he leaves all the doors open, even the front door. A blue dusky light penetrates my room and out-of-doors I can hear an uproar—grinding, screeching, grating, singing, whistling.

Never have I dressed more quickly. Out in the open, through the small hole in the snow, an icy damp mist envelops the dull reddish twilight. Before me, where the dark waters of the bay and sea used to stretch, there is now a tremendous white mass of pack ice as far as the eye can reach. In an irresistible regular movement the gigantic ice floes are driving forward, boulders of ice piled high on top of each other, thickly covered in snow and looking like mountains that have wandered down here into our bay from the north. Rumbling and thundering, the huge blocks of ice crash into each other, and further out the sea is roaring on a single shrill prolonged note.

We stand there in the midst of this titanic drama. There is movement and life again. A feeling of boundless joy overwhelms all three of us, as though the stream of life were suddenly flowing through us again after a long paralysis. None of us thinks of a proper breakfast. Karl is cleaning his gun as though possessed, and Hermann laces up his *komaga* while he writes up his weather report. The coffee grows cold in the cups. Finally they slip on their anoraks, take their guns, and go out. They go right away in different directions and disappear in the distance into the dusky, icy landscape.

I am left alone in the snow. I feel as though I had suddenly been set down in a large, alien city whose language I do not understand. But I cannot stay in the hut today. It is dull and silent under the snow. A tidy and well-run household has no interest for me.

With an enormous Colt in my belt, I venture out to the tip of our little promontory. There, with my back to the woodpile, I watch the performance of the moving ice.

The entire vast stream, once set in motion by the wind and the sea's current, moves with an irresistible force, ignoring obstacles. Where the bays of Grey Hook lie open to the north, the ice floes push against the steep frozen banks and, piling up, spill over onto the land. With my field glasses I look out to sea. Everywhere, right up to the horizon, the ice masses are on the move.

Now I can grasp the power of the ice. Now I can get an idea of what it means for a ship to be caught in its embrace. What a superhuman struggle it must demand to save one's life from those crushing drifting masses. Whoever gets caught is lost. In the course of centuries a host of ships have been ground to pieces against these coasts by the ice. Jammer Bay, Sorge Bay, Bangen Hook—now I understand the names.

5 February. Twenty-two degrees below zero. A windless day. The ice is lying tightly packed in the bay, although not yet frozen right over. Patches of dark open water can still be seen here and there.

6 February. Today the first bear came. He climbed the cliffs by the shore onto the land close by our hut. He came apparently across the sea ice, and his tracks led to the boat whose dark keel was sticking out of the snow. Unfortunately we were not at home. Karl had gone early to Odden, and I had accompanied Hermann to the mountains. I came home earlier than him to get the dinner ready. Karl returned only late in the evening. He had noticed the fresh bear tracks on his way home and had followed them inland by the fjord. He said the bear had struck the heavy stones from all the fox traps and eaten the bait, sticks and all.

We go out looking for my husband, who had given me his gun in the morning so that I might have a weapon for the trip home. We find him at the entrance to Wijde Bay. Karl thinks that the bear is still in Grey Hook; it will be our bear. But Hermann thinks it will not come back, for bears are restless wanderers. Judging from the tracks it was a small bear, although the marks of the paws seem huge and our footprints, by contrast, no bigger than those of dolls.

Hastily we start to set spring-gun traps. They strike me as extremely primitive. They are made of empty boxes—we used a couple of empty orange boxes—resting on four posts. Some fat, some wire, and a small revolver are enough to bring down a beast as big as that. The spring guns are set upon rocky spits of land and surrounded by a ring of stakes, which can be seen from far out to sea. These arouse the curiosity of the animals and they come ashore to inspect them; everything is then made easy for them to find their way to the piece of fat. This is placed in the box at about the height of the animal's head. When the bear approaches the trap, the gun is fired and the bullet enters its head.

Several of these traps are set up. One on Odden, a few further along the coast, and two in the neighbourhood of our hut. Some seal fat is put on the fire, so that when the wind blows toward the sea the smell of the burning fat attracts the bears to the coast and so to the traps.

These preparations for murder are ill-suited to the bewitching return of the light. In the gentle twilight hues of tender pink and greenish-blue the moon is still shining, and the bright veils of the northern lights are still floating hither and thither over the dawn-bright sky.

Scarcely is the last trap set—it is cold work and takes a lot of time—than a whistling and cracking starts up at the fjord. Long, drawn hissing sounds come and go between the shore and the sea. There is a gurgling and rumbling under the heavy blanket of ice. In the night the wind blows from the south, a melancholy humming. By morning, to our great disgust and astonishment, all the ice has been driven out of the bay.

15 February. Wind from the southwest. Five degrees above zero. Everything is thawing, and drops are trickling from the roof. We have to bury the potatoes in the snow to prevent them thawing, and we have also, unfortunately, to eat up our last eider duck at one sitting. "It's the infernal gulf stream," says Karl, cursing the warmth blown over to us from the western sea.

16 February. Thirty-five degrees below and a north wind. The ice comes back into the bay. The eider ducks have returned to our shore. But we are no longer looking for small birds; now that bears have reached our coast, we have higher ambitions.

The continuing icy wind freezes the fjord. The pack ice is locked in the bay. A strange new landscape takes shape around our peninsula. Through the mighty jagged arches and towers of ice piled up in wild caprice the storm rages, and the driving snow builds new and fantastic giants. When the weather clears, the sea has become a white rigid wilderness of ice floes, as far as the eye can reach. In the clear air the distant horizon is sharply outlined in jagged peaks. A deceptive calm lies over everything. A patch of dawn red floats in the pastel blue sky. In the distance I can see the two men at work, small as ants against the titanic landscape. They are repairing the fox traps that the bear had destroyed.

Karl returns alone. My husband has gone further down the fjord, intending to return by noon tomorrow. But now it is evening and he is not yet back, and gradually we both get anxious. It is dark, and a thick mist is lying over everything. Then there is a shot from the direction of the sea. We run out, and there is a second shot. Now we know. He has lost his way. Now Karl fires a shot too, to give Hermann his bearings.

A long time passes, full of apprehension. There are still cracks and holes in the ice. Then our calls are answered, and soon a figure completely covered in hoarfrost clambers over the bank. Hermann had tried a shortcut across a bay and in the darkness had lost his way.

20 February. The men are tired of shovelling snow. They have made a brilliant discovery. They have shovelled a path in the snow from the outer door toward the north, from which direction the least snow is driven. The path is roofed over with beams, and a few steps cut into the snow lead out into the open. When we are in the hut the opening is protected by cases laid on top of each other. Now the snow can fall as much as it likes, and it will still be easy for us to get out into the open. Apart from that the path gives us more space. In its white walls we

cut out niches for the coal sacks, the potatoes, and the box of salted meat. We have a snow-white storeroom.

25 February. We are all in a holiday mood today, for we shall see the sun again for the first time. The sky is clear except to the south, where an arc of clouds reflects at its edges the light of the sun. The frozen land is still lying in bluish-grey shadow. More gleaming clouds rise over the horizon, throwing long dark shadows into the banks of mist to the north. One strip of ice is already glittering in the sun.

Below, on the furthermost tip of Wood Bay, there is a gap between the high mountains. That is where we saw the sun for the last time, and that is where it will first shine again. We are standing on the ice of the sea, following the shining light stretching behind the chain of mountains. There! A bright light flashes out between the mountains; then the reflection moves further westward. For a second we have seen the sun.

A gull comes flying in down the fjord. The first gull to return. It is flying very high, but when it sees us it swoops down lower, circles round us, and flies off again.

The frozen world lies in untouched beauty, in holy quiet. With wings beating slowly, the bird flies under the glowing heavens across the fjord, as though it were the first living thing to take possession of a newly created, untouched, magnificent world.

13

A Dead Land

The tension and excitement of the pack ice, the joy of the returning light, are followed by a period of profound sobriety. Now there is too much ice, say the hunters, and that is why all the animals are keeping away.

Looking round us from the top of the hills we can see an immense girdle of pack ice circling the north coast, with no open water. Bears and seals, however, are to be found only where there is open water. There is no trace of an animal in Grey Hook. The outlook for hunting is bad, and the men are silent and grave.

The light, a thin misty white light, illuminates the vast and unbroken deadness around us. Almost we feel a longing for the darkness, for the deep unknowing obscurity with its shining dreams and its waiting for the return of life.

Karl has gone into the interior down Wijde Bay to collect the foxes from the traps. Hermann wants to get to Cape Roos across the ice. They are both hoping that some living creature will cross the path of their guns, providing us at last with the vitamins for which we are longing.

Karl starts off at the end of February; I shall never forget the beauty of the morning twilight. My husband will accompany him for a short part of the way, carrying the heavy rucksack. The whole sky is deep lilac, lightening into a tender cobalt blue at the horizon, over the sea of ice. From the east a pale-yellow brightness spreads, and the frozen sea, reflecting the heavenly colours, shines like an immense opal. Where sea and land meet, and where the tidal water thrusts through to the surface around the heavy masses of ice, the colours of the sky are reflected as brightly as in a mirror.

I stand a long time in front of the hut, immersed in the intoxicating beauty of the scene. Suddenly I hear a voice quite close to my ear. "Go left up the slope; there's always some there." Astonished, I turn round. There is not a soul to be seen. The men have long since vanished from my sight. "Then at least you'll have fresh meat," the ghost voice in the air continues. "For us out here things will soon get critical."

"So long." The reply, coming out of the air, seems to be in Karl's voice. "At least I'll bring you back some fresh ptarmigan." Then I can hear the sound of skis, but I cannot tell whether they are approaching or receding. Then a sudden silence, which is not broken.

I go on standing there a long time, waiting, and thinking that the men must have turned back and that in a moment I will see them, quite close. But they do not return, and after a while it dawns on me that I have had the same experience before, of voices being carried over long distances; it is a phenomenon that occurs in the clear air of the high north.

I return to the hut. Its air of neglect and the muddy dirt leer at me from every corner. I can control myself no longer; there is nobody here to forbid me, and before my own common sense can raise any objection to the insane first step, I have covered the whole room in boiling suds: I set about scrubbing with a really savage pleasure.

When my husband comes home, the water on the walls and floor has frozen. The whole hut is sparking like a crystal palace. "Are you mad?" Hermann cries out.

"Better mad in a clean hut than sane in a pigsty," I retort, and go on scrubbing. No power in the world can stay my scouring jag. Whether it is a reaction from the depression of the long night, or whether every woman in the world has an uncontrollable urge to spring-clean after the winter, I do not know. Hermann storms, I storm; we have a terrific set-to. All the stored-up nerviness of the winter night erupts in a sudden explosion. I am astonished at my own violence, of which I had never known myself capable in Europe.

As great as its fury is the peace that follows the storm. Lighthearted and singing we go each about our work. Hermann gets everything ready to make a Nansen sleigh for his contemplated trip, and I go on scrubbing. I come across a mattress that is mildewed and wringing wet on the underside. I drag it out to the snow hole. An icy wind is blowing. In a fit of rage, and with hands paralysed by the cold, I tear off the cover. At once the strips of linen freeze as stiff as boards which, caught by the wind, go clattering down to the sea, where they bob up and down like black figures between the ice floes and then disappear into the magical violet of the surrounding scene. For days afterward there was much puzzled speculation about the origin of the curious marks they left in the snow.

Only when the store cupboard has been scoured clean of the snow that has found its way in through the doors and cracks am I satisfied. Now we have a bright and shining hut.

When the Nansen sleigh is finished, my husband and I get ready for the trip down the fjord. He wants to collect the foxes from the Wood Bay area as well as from Cape Roos. Karl, it is true, has tried to dissuade us from making the trip over the frozen fjord because of the notoriously dangerous currents there, but Hermann has been given detailed and precise directions for the journey by the hunter Nois, who has often made the same trip. There is no holding Hermann, and I have begged to be taken at least as far as the hut on Svendsen Bay.

It is a fine day when we prepare to set off. Out-of-doors we load up the sleigh with all the essentials for our journey—sleeping bags, gun, saw and axe, bait sticks, and the tools to repair and erect the traps. Altogether it makes a pretty substantial load.

When everything has been stowed and made fast, sailor fashion, we go back to the warm hut. When taking this rest, which is customary among the hunters before a difficult winter journey and which affects the novice almost like a devotional exercise, a last hot drink is taken, slowly, while in full marching kit. No superfluous word is spoken. Every thought and all the body's strength are concentrated on the coming expedition. We realise quite clearly that on the trip we are making today we will not be able to take a rest. With the temperature thirty-eight degrees below, and with the wind, even a few minutes spent without bodily movement are dangerous for warm-blooded men.

The door of the hut is rammed to; we slip on our skis, and trailing the packed sleigh, we race down the steep escarpment onto the sea of ice. The sleigh is attached to a leather belt that my husband wears round his chest. Moving behind him, I try with the tip of my ski to push the sleigh forward.

At first we go at a moderate pace over the surface of powdered snow, but soon we meet a headwind, the ice becomes uneven, and we have to find a path for the sleigh over and between the jutting ice floes. At last, after about an hour of travelling, the sleigh is held up among the jumble of ice boulders, and we can get it no further. We have no choice but to carry it back up the steep slope of the shore and continue our journey on land.

To me it seems that we are making only slow progress round the foot of the towering Rillenberg Range. It takes many hundred steps to go round each spur of the mountain. I no longer push the sleigh forward. Deliberately I stay a little in the rear, and now and again I lift the protecting woollen scarf from my face. Cape Roos and the frozen-over Bock Bay lie before us. The mountains in the distance, the fjord, and the tremendous mass of the Rillenberg beside us are all glittering and sparkling in the incomparable brightness of the rosy morning sun.

The unprotected human eye can stand the frozen splendour only for a few seconds. In its clearness the dazzling land seems so palpable, and yet its inexpressibly motionless quiet makes it remote and strange, as though it has been forgotten for thousands of years, submerged in ice-clear depths of water.

Surreptitiously I rummage in the moving sleigh for my small camera. It seems to me a deadly sin to steal a piece of this supernatural scene and carry it away with me. Nor can I do so, for the camera case will not open. It is jammed. Apparently the oil in the mechanism has frozen, and so too have my hands, bared for a moment and now snow white.

My husband turns round. He rubs my hands between his warm ones with a fury that makes me want to howl with pain. Then, when life has returned to them, he puts on my gloves, winds my scarf around my face, and without a word continues on his way. I feel that I have been reprimanded, like an ill-behaved, stupid child. Behind my woollen veil, condemned to semi-blindness, I trot along behind the sleigh.

Wind from the valleys, blowing between the mountains, beats about us. Our road goes on over the steep frozen slopes, along the frozen cliffs of the shore; sometimes I slip up to my hips into snow-filled crevasses. On and on. No rest is permitted. I cannot complain; I asked to be taken on the trip. Nor could I utter a word of complaint. The immense silence of the land surrounds me and invades me, submerging and annihilating my human smallness.

Hours later we reach the little tongue of land that juts out into Svendsen Bay where there is a small hut. It is buried under snow; only the black stovepipe rises above the white surface. Our first job is to shovel the snow away from the hut. Inside, Karl, who was the last to use it in the autumn, has left everything ready for the next comer as the hunters of Spitsbergen do: dry kindling and logs in front of the stove, and everything clean. We are happy to emerge gradually from our frozen shells. Sitting by the small glowing stove, comfortably wrapped in thick sheepskin rugs, we eat an eider duck caught the summer before and left hanging in the hut for winter supplies. The rich soup does us an enormous amount of good.

My husband is silent. Through the tiny window of the hut we can see the broad frozen surface of Wood Bay. Over our whole field of vision the ice of the fjord stretches high and jagged, the floes piled up on top of each other, leaving sharp chasms between. Here the mountains along the coast fall so steeply into the sea that they are no use for walking. We can only go on by crossing the fjord, but there the surface is so tumbled and broken that it is impossible to make a path for the sleigh. If Hermann is to continue his trip, he has no option but to carry the load on his back. He takes with him only the most essential equipment for his overnight stay in huts that are not prepared for his coming. Even so it makes a pretty heavy burden, with the body's strength reduced as it is by the winter night.

The next day I watch him disappear, the load piled high on his back, a moving black speck in the distance, vanishing among the ice floes. By this time I have learnt what I must do when I am alone—work, and go on working, to make the cold and the solitude tolerable. By the shore, close to the hut, are the supplies of driftwood gathered in the previous year; they have been piled up like a pyramid, and the tips are sticking out of the snow. The smaller pieces and logs, which I can carry, I dig out of the snow and drag to the hut. I work the whole day, unthinking and without a wish, like a draught animal that must work to live.

The next day I start sawing the wood. The sawing block, with which every hut is provided, has to be dug out of the snow; the saw itself is in the hut. Maybe it is a peculiar quality of the clear air, maybe it is a peculiarity of the wood, dried by years of wind and sun—I do not know; but I can go on sawing for hours without getting tired. Splitting the logs is a problem, for the axe in the hut is so blunt that it just recoils from the wood without splitting it.

I search the hut, which is no bigger than a bunk in length and about the same in width, for something with which to sharpen the axe.

A number of remarkable things come to light. A large rusty compass lamp, a number of broken bits of a ship's parts, and three gorgeous porcelain dishes with broad gold rims and a monogram, which have probably found their way here from some abandoned coal mine managed by a person of title. I have to laugh over the collector's mania of the people here, who like foxes carry to their earths every unclaimed article. Only later emergencies can tell whether the things are of any use.

I also find various messages that the hunters always leave before setting out on a long journey, to facilitate the search for them if they are thought to be lost. And there are notes scribbled also on the walls and on the white border of a large map of Sweden, hung on the thin wall to keep out the draught. They read like brief self-communings: thoughts about storms, fog, and darkness. More than one lonely hunter, forced perhaps to take shelter in the little hut, wanted to communicate his thoughts if only to the walls, to prove that he was still alive.

I also find a stone, with which I whet the axe. I spend a whole day on this job, and in the evening it splits the wood. The next evening there is a pretty good pile of split logs inside the hut, and another outside.

Now, when the most essential work has been done, and I no longer grudge the time to take a rest in the hut, anxiety comes creeping in. The bright confidence, the optimism, which inspires a man when he is working, has gone. Will Hermann have found the way across the fjord that bypasses the holes in the ice formed by the current? As far as I know, this journey has never been made on foot before, without dog sleigh. The hunters frequently tell stories of their comrades disappearing without a trace in the ice of the fjords. And how will he manage, after the hard travelling, in the huts, not all of which are stoked with supplies, and perhaps also without a store of wood for fuel? Many of the huts, according to Karl, are in such bad condition that "the scene looks in through the walls."

To these anxieties about my husband I add anxiety about my own welfare. I have discovered to my horror that there are no matches in the case of stores, and in the box I have brought with me there are only three matches left. How will I be able to manage for fourteen days with only three matches? If the drift snow starts to blow, I will not be able to break up the wood outside the hut to keep the fire going day and night. Nor, if the snow starts falling, or fog comes down, will it be possible for me to make my way back to Grey Hook.

So I make up my mind to take advantage of the fine weather and to start alone early the next morning for Grey Hook. With a remarkable calm, bestowed on people up here when they are still masters of their own decisions, I read the Norwegian *Familienjournal*, a favourite of the Spitsbergen hunters, with its gay caricatures and simple jokes, and which can be found in every hut, even if it is often years old and the print practically rubbed off from so much reading.

Suddenly, breaking through all other pictures, I see my husband coming back across the ice. I go out of the hut and from the door I really can see him, a moving black speck in the distance, making his way between the maze of boulders.

There is still time to put soup on the fire, to lay the small table, and to go a good way to meet him on the ice with the

Nansen sleigh. With a sigh of relief he lets his heavy rucksack fall. At first all he can say is "Impossible." Then he says that he had managed to get down into Wood Bay but could not reach Cape Roos. The ice was salty, and at last became so thin that he had to turn back.

How happy I am that he has come back unhurt. We will gladly give up the foxes if in return we keep our lives.

The next day we return to Grey Hook. The weather is mild, only twelve degrees below; to us it seems so warm that the sweat trickles down our faces. The snow sticks to our feet, the misty air makes breathing difficult. "Mild weather like this is the worst enemy you can have up here when you're travelling these distances," my husband asserts.

Dead tired I drag along to Grey Hook. But Hermann is so lively that the very next day he starts off for Biscay Hook, where Sven Ohlson, our only neighbour, is spending the winter. Over there, far to the west, Hermann hopes to get some hunting in open water, to supply me with fresh meat before he starts on his yearly journey to the radio station in Advent Anchorage, where he will send news home and collect the mail. While he is away I shall be alone for weeks in the hut.

The road to Sven Ohlson crosses Wood Bay and goes along the north coast over Rode Bay. Before leaving, Hermann gives me the last piece of frozen fox meat, with strict instructions to eat it all up.

I have now been alone for nine days. Hermann did not say how long he would be away. Out-of-doors the country lies white, rigid, and absolutely quiet. There is not a breath of wind.

Our little wind-torn weathervane has frozen fast to its pole. The storms have receded. To the furthest distance stretches the ice. The atmosphere is so even there is no reason for the air to move.

But for humans this stillness is horrible. It is days since I have been outside the hut. Gradually I have become fearful of seeing the deadness of the land. I sit in the hut and tire myself out with sewing. It makes no difference whether the work is finished today or tomorrow, but I know what I'm up to. I do not want to have my mind free for a moment to think, a moment in which to become aware of the nothingness outside. I have become conscious of the power of thought, a power that up here can bestow life or death. I have an inkling, or rather I know with certainty that it was this, this terror of nothingness that over the past centuries has been responsible for the death of some hundreds of men here in Spitsbergen.

It wasn't only scurvy. Often enough they died though the larders were full and there was plenty of fresh meat. They had guns and cartridges; there were reindeer grazing in all the valleys. But they did not dare to venture out. The terror lay in wait for them just outside the door of the hut; it sprawled over the entire bleak land like a monster. It riveted the most courageous hunters and seafarers to their hut. It was the image of the immense deadness of the country, the fearful immobility of all being that had been graven in their souls, crippling all their energies and emptying them of strength. Physical disintegration was bound to follow.

The Spitsbergen hunters today are different. To the deadness they oppose their vitality. They journey alone through the desolate land, without fear of its stillness, its storms, or its night. They journey for miles, putting up a hard fight for their earnings, in order to be able to stay again for one more year here in the high north.

To keep myself from thoughts of my loneliness I read my husband's diary, and I get some idea of the most extreme experiences the country provides, which I, as the timid guardian of a hut, will never quite grasp.

In the diary there are accounts of his trips in an open boat hundreds of miles along the coast, and of his lonely expeditions across the country, which is so beautiful and so full of lurking dangers. Trips across glaciers, with their glimpse northward across the sea and southward across the fjords; trips across sunny, frozen bays, the grotesquely shaped mountains, armoured in ice, gleaming in the sun; marches along the wall-like mountain massif on a narrow frozen path, the treacherous freshly fallen snow on one side and on the other the sheer drop of the mountains cut by numberless fissures, the paths marked out by avalanches of rock and ice. I read about his forced halts in tiny huts without windows, where the stoves smoke and the lamps smoulder, in notorious huts where the wind tears through the half-destroyed frames, and small wooden crosses mark the graves of those who died of scurvy.

He has written also of coming to comfortable huts and being welcomed by hunters who have lived many months alone, of the joy of exchanging news, of the friendliness of the Norwegians and of their unfailing and unreserved hospitality. Hermann's journeys have taken him over frozen mountain ranges when the dangerous state of the ice in the fjords forced him to make detours; he has scrambled over the ice inland, with gusts of snow driving at hurricane force down between the walls of cliff, thrusting clouds of snow before them like waterfalls. Sometimes, up on the heights, for days on end the whirling snow reduced visibility to nil. Then down across the glaciers and on along the rocky shore from which, through the mist, can be heard the thunder of the ice as it breaks up and the surging of the sea.

He has taken trips in the winter night, crossing by moonlight the glittering mountains and frozen lagoons from which rise spectrally the pale roots of gigantic Siberian trees brought in by the tides. The storms break suddenly and the moon is darkened. In the immense roaring darkness and frightful cold, feeling his way across the endless slopes and the ravines filled with snowdrifts, it is really only the reawakened primitive instinct of the homing animal that enables him to find his way back to the rescuing hut.

The lives of these hunters are a series of performances that are almost inhuman. But they speak only seldom of their experiences. They are not out for fame, these men. They live far from the tumult of the world. Practically none of them has a home or a family. It is an unbounded love that chains them to the country. They are intoxicated by the vital breath of untamed nature, through which the deity speaks to them.

I put away the little books, which are full to bursting with intense experience and an unfailing and unbounded stream of vigour. I feel ashamed of being too cowardly to look out on the land, where these others struggle throughout their lives in darkness and storm. Summoning all my energy, I force myself to go out of doors. There is no movement in the land, lying dead still in the dreaming cobalt blue of the bright night. A pale-yellow light circles the earth. I can see the reflection of the sun as it wanders across the Atlantic, across America, and across the Pacific Ocean.

This is the tenth day of my being alone. Last night I had a fearful dream. Although no one has ever told me about it, I now know how powerful is the attraction of the water flowing under the ice. I saw the green water under the ice and felt physically its power to entice.

I am anxious about Hermann.

Eleven days alone. I have hacked away some of the hard frozen snow hill in front of the window, and now I can look out toward the ice of the sea.

The twelfth day. There are mirages outside. Ice from the frozen sea at the horizon has risen up and poised itself upside down on the peaks of the jagged surface. A tall white colonnade seems to be rushing eastward, moving with the warmer currents of air from the west. The flat hills of Verlegen Hook, stretching far out into the sea in the east, have also grown taller. Their lower slopes seem to have broken into zigzag lines. Mirages are the most infallible sign of a change in the weather.

Thirteenth day. The day passes as though it were no more than an hour. Is it because I have only one anxiety?

Fourteenth day. I no longer look out across the ice; the lifeless rigidity is too frightful.

On the sixteenth day there is a shot outside, and when I crawl out of the hole in the snow I see the tiny black figure on the ice, slowly drawing nearer to our coast. It is my husband returning, burnt dark and terribly thin; and with empty hands. Over at Sven's also the sea is iced right up, and no living creature has yet appeared. But Sven has sent a small bag of dried onions for the lady, which are supposed to contain vitamins.

It took Hermann a day and a half to reach Biscay Hook, without any possibility of rest, a distance of forty miles of very hard going. Ignorant of the danger, he had crossed the notorious Russenstrom, a narrow channel of water connecting an inland lake with the sea. The powerful current there, which flows perpetually, never allows an ice surface to form, but the water is often covered with treacherous snowdrifts, as Sven later told him.

Sven's joy at the visit was indescribable. After resting in Sven's hut for two days, and after a further two days' involuntary stay in the hut because of a storm, the two hunters then took off together with the dogs for the reindeer district of Odden. There they separated, but only found tracks of reindeer in the southern part of the peninsula. Neither of them brought anything down. But Sven has promised to come over to us as soon as he has got a seal or a bear, to bring us fresh meat.

At the beginning of April Karl returns, also very thin and burnt dark. In Wijde Bay, too, everything is dead; apart from two ptarmigan, he has shot nothing. But he does bring back a sleigh full of fox pelts. Physical exhaustion can be read on his face, but his eyes are shining with gladness because he is again with other people. He has been alone for two months.

14

A Hunter Brings the Mail

Today, 12 April, something quite out of the ordinary happens. It is a winter day of perfect beauty, the light over the still and frozen land is almost hard in its clarity. For some days now the thermometer has been steady at thirty-five degrees below. It is the first day on which hoarfrost does not settle on everything at the least breath of wind. So the two hunters hang out their white fox pelts in the sun, to dry them and bleach them. The sun and the wind make the hair loose and silky. But first the pelts have to be treated with sawdust and benzine, and the hut once again looks like a stable. Out-of-doors Hermann is building a frame of skis and ski sticks on which the pelts are to be hung. Suddenly he taps on the window and calls Karl and me out. "Listen," he says, his face beaming.

In the great quiet, as yet distant but still quite unmistakable, we can hear a human voice: "Hoyee, hoyee…" it is calling. It can only be a hunter with a dog sleigh. And then, on the slope under the mountains of Grey Hook, the sleigh comes into sight, looking like a tiny black toy. In front five racing black dogs and behind two upright figures. Hermann recognises the team; it belongs to his old friend Nois, the hunter who built our hut; he is accompanied by one of his assistants. In a bold sweep the team drives up before the hut, men and dogs rimed with frost. We are overjoyed at seeing people again, and Nois is delighted at finding all three of us, whom he has wanted to visit, fit and well. We shake hands all round. "Welcome, welcome, *takk for sist.*" *Takk for sist*—thanks for the last time—is a customary greeting among friends in Norway.

Hilmar Nois, who has lived on the island as a hunter for twenty-five years, for whom no enterprise is too bold, no trouble too great if it is a question of giving help, is the typical Norwegian hunter in appearance. Tall, broad-shouldered, his face burnt brown, light eyes, light eyelashes, and bushy eyebrows. His clothes, like the clothes of all who winter here, are a yellowish-white and clumsily mended with large patches, and on his feet—you wouldn't think it possible that one could go through the Spitsbergen winter in this footwear—he has only thick socks, to which have been sewn soles made of pieces of raw rubber. He and his companion are freshly shaven.

Smiling, Nois looks at his hut, sunk deep under snow, and at the frozen sea. "You've got enough pack ice out here."

His companion, a lanky young man, unharnesses the dogs and throws down to each of them a piece of frozen meat. In the hut, Nois brings out of his rucksack an enormous packet of letters and radio-telegrams. We throw ourselves on them and read them and sigh with relief. "Thank God, everything at home is all right." Meanwhile, Nois sits down at the little table by the window and seizes happily on the pack of cards lying there and at once loses himself in a game of patience. He makes absolutely nothing of having undertaken a journey of several days in order to visit us and bring us our mail; from his headquarters' hut in Sassendal, and making a detour to pick up the mail, he has travelled one hundred and seventy-five miles across glaciers and fjords.

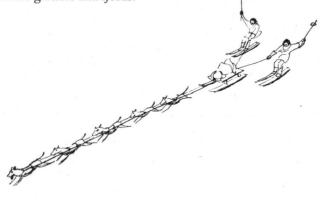

"Tell us, Nois," says Hermann, "what's happening in the world? Is there a war?"

Nois is absorbed in his game of patience. His replies are brief and mumbled.

"War? No, not yet."

"And how about the price of foxes?"

"Bad."

"Is Spitsbergen already divided up into hunting grounds?"

"No, the devil knows."

Bit by bit, however, we get to hear all the news and the latest Spitsbergen gossip. Although only a few quite solitary men live scattered along the coast, gossip is as welcome as in a small town, except that all incidents are even more exaggerated, considering the great distances. Soon the conversation is flowing as fast as a millstream.

It transpires that Nois' companion is a doctor, a parasitologist by profession, who has spent the winter with Nois and who, to his great grief, has found nothing even approaching a parasite in reindeer or seals or foxes. All his hopes are now centred on our foxes.

Now the conversation grows even more animated, for Hermann has learnt that during the winter the doctor has listened in to the news from Europe. Although he had been satisfied with Nois' meagre statement that there was no war anywhere, he is still restless and wants to hear more.

We get a full report. One question leads to another. Long discussions ensue, and soon the hut is shadowed by the gloomy clouds of the stormy European sky, under which the two men pace gravely up and down. I see again the anxious face of Europe, which here I had quite forgotten.

But Karl and Nois, with the happiest faces in the world, are telling funny stories about their seafaring and hunting lives, and laughing loudly. They have something of the gaiety and simplicity of primitive peoples whose lives are closely bound to nature and who have not lost themselves in the fine-spun intellectualisms of the civilised world. They have the faces of untroubled boys.

The contrast in the aspect of the two worlds, so close to each other, is striking. And suddenly I realise that civilisation is suffering from a severe vitamin deficiency because it cannot draw its strength directly from nature, eternally young and eternally true. Humanity has lost itself in the unnatural and in speculation. Only now do I grasp the real meaning and the world-transforming element in the saying: "Become as the peasants, understand the sacredness of the earth."

Our midday meal is, unfortunately, scarcely festive. It is as monotonous as our stores. We tell Nois about our bad luck in getting no fresh meat.

"Yes, Grey Hook is a dead place. But at Easter you will all be my guests at Sassendalhytta. I shot plenty of ptarmigan and I've kept a pot of orange marmalade for you. And my glass verandah is also finished."

To my great astonishment I learn that in two days' time we shall all go south with Nois' dog sleigh, according to an arrangement with Nois that my husband had made last year, in the autumn, to get the first ship returning home.

Greatly as home attracts me, I can scarcely grasp that we are to leave this country so suddenly. But I do not want to interfere with the men's plans, and so I too begin to get ready for the journey.

There is still a great deal to be done. Clearing up and looking for things and packing. The visitors help as much as they can. Nois skins the last fox, which is immediately seized by the doctor, who dissects it. It is difficult to understand how all this can be done in a room measuring ten feet square, with all four men unusually big and broad-shouldered. To add to it all, the big shaggy Jumbo, a quarrelsome dog that must be kept apart from the others, is sitting in the middle of the hut and getting in everyone's way.

But we manage. We are all in the best of tempers. Nois even finds it madly comfortable here, and says that whatever happens he too will keep a kitchen maid next year. He can see for himself how nice it will be.

The doctor's joy is indescribable when he brings to light a tapeworm, which he solemnly puts on my kitchen table. Then he carries on with his dissecting, for who knows how many valuable surprises this priceless fox conceals.

All the fox traps in the neighbourhood have still to be dismantled. Nois set his dogs to help with the job, and at the same time I am to get my training in *ski-kjöring* for the long journey. First we go down by the fjord.

The sleigh is ready; the shaggy black dogs have been harnessed, one behind the other. The driving rein runs through the harness.

"Hold on tight, lady," says Nois, putting into my hand a rope made fast to the sleigh. Then "Hoiho," he cries.

With a sudden jerk all five dogs start off together and race away, carrying along everything behind them willy-nilly over the frozen hillocks and hollows. Then the whole column suddenly halts. One of the dogs has a little business to do. "Hoiho." Again we race over the ice and stones. Again everything stops, as though at a word of command. The leading dog wants a break, and so it goes on until none of the dogs has an excuse any longer to call a halt. These are the incidents of a sleigh journey that you don't read of in books about the Arctic, I think to myself. After that, however, we work up a fine speed over a stretch of level ground. Uphill the pace is a little slower, but even so they go at a pretty good trot. "Keep up with them," Hermann calls out. "Keep your pace even," the doctor shouts. "Keep your knees bent. Push off with your stick." I try to follow all the instructions and still to keep my balance. The dogs are given the direction by shouts of "Left", "Right". They obey the spoken word. The leading dog is so intelligent that he seems to know in advance what to do. We come to a canyon, a riverbed cut into the rocks. Snow has drifted into cornices over the steep rocky sides, but in places the drift has closed over the gap and it seems possible to cross. At sight of the canyon the dogs put on an extra spurt, which carries them across to the other side. The dogs have managed it, but I am down in the canyon.

Now and again, while the traps are being dismantled, I have to sit on the sleigh and take a rest. Around us Spitsbergen is dazzling in its white immensity and splendour. Today the temperature is fifteen degrees below, and to us it feels warm.

In dream-like quietness the mighty hills surround us, in their midst the frozen fjord under its glittering rumpled blanket of ice floes. The dogs are lying down peacefully, biting at the ice between their toes. They are obviously glad to have a rest. When, continuing our journey, the dogs catch sight of the little Svendsen Bay hut, and the driver urges them on with cries of "*Hytta, hytta*", they know that they are coming to the end and race as hard as they can.

The hut is once again barred by snowdrifts and has to be shovelled clear. The dogs settle down in the soft snow in the sun. I get a snack ready in the hut. There is enough tea, sugar, condensed milk, rusks, and butter.

The doctor is surprised at my healthy looks and my "incomparable peace of mind". Is it not so wonderful when, as here, we are engaged in our daily round only on what is absolutely essential to life, and there is time, day and night, to live in nature? As we go on with our conversation, we find ourselves pitying all the people in the towns of Europe, particularly the housewives, who besides being worn out by the unending struggle against soot and dust, moths and mice, also feel themselves obliged to keep up appearances. And then we talk about the aesthetic pleasures of Europe, which when we were there seemed so priceless to us—music, for example, that elevates the mind and lightens the heart and without which we could hardly live. Remarkably enough, the hunger for music is quite absent here. Our hearts are light, our minds are in a permanent state of elevation. Nature seems to contain everything that man needs for his equilibrium.

Outside, meanwhile, the dogs have dug out of the snow all the eider duck skins we threw away last autumn and have eaten them, which is something they should not have done. Having eaten too much, they are strongly disinclined to make the pull on the homeward trip. They drop again and again into a slow trot, turn aside when the road goes upward, and behave altogether just as if they had never heard the words "left" and "right".

Being drawn along in this uneven way is, of course, much more of a strain on one's legs than the smooth following of a regular pace. Only when we come to a height where our road leads down a steep slope do the dogs work up some enthusiasm. The two men do their best to brake the sleigh and keep us away from the left side, where the hill falls sheer into the sea. They just manage it. But when we reach the valley at the foot of the hill the sleigh overturns, the dogs get tangled in the harness, and end up by biting and snapping at each other.

It takes some time to get the dogs separated; first of all their paws have to be sorted out from the tangle of harness, a job that the two perspiring men at last accomplish. Then we go on for a time at a peaceful run; the dogs patter along evenly and neatly. I am perched high up on the packed sleigh, and it is all I can do to keep my balance as we bump across the ice and the rocks. We reach our hut at last.

．　　．　　．

We all go early to bed, for we have a hard trip ahead of us the next day. When everything in the hut is still, I creep out once more through the hole in the snow to take leave of Grey Hook.

It is a beautiful, still, and holy night, earth and sky shadowed in a tender cobalt blue. The frozen slopes of the mountains and the coast have no reality; they are a dream lit up by the soft and hazy yellow light of the sun's reflection as it moves round the northern horizon. And over everything the calm that elsewhere inheres only in the world beyond our own.

Some of the dogs are lying on the roof of the hut, the others in the snow. One of them slowly rises, his black coat rimed with frost. He looks at me with large serious eyes, asking nothing and saying nothing, remote from the world and from reality, and yet full of a deep and dreaming life, the same secret life that seems to be hidden everywhere in this quiet land.

Noiselessly I crawl back into the hut. Everything is quiet there. They are all asleep. I lie awake a long time, although I am dead tired. I know that I won't go with them tomorrow on their journey. I can't… I simply can't go away from here. I know that it will become still more beautiful when the animals return and everything awakens to life. I decide to stay here alone, if my husband insists on making the trip to Advent Anchorage.

The next day I tell the men of my decision. A general silence. Then Karl breaks out. "Spitsbergen mania. Spitsbergen mania. Now the lady's gone mad." Then they start persuading me, as though I were a sick horse.

"You can make the whole trip on my sleigh," says Nois, who thinks I am afraid of the long journey.

"I can't take the responsibility of leaving you alone here on the coast without vitamins," says the doctor. "This is your last chance to make the trip."

"Spitsbergen mania," Karl says over and over again.

Only my husband says nothing. He understands. He himself will never get away from Spitsbergen.

At last the others start off, and Karl goes with them. As Hermann is again going to spend the next winter alone, Karl has taken a job for the summer, which Nois has offered him, and has to go to Tromsø. It is hard to say goodbye to this loyal and devoted comrade of the winter night, whose kind heart and unfailing good humour we will never forget. Karl promises to write to us for the rest of his life. The doctor promises to send us the political news with the first fishing vessel, and Nois says he intends to come up here in his motorboat to collect down. Then he will bring us vegetables, and he will have his father with him, who asked for a trip by boat round Spitsbergen for his seventieth birthday.

We shake hands and thank them. Then "Hoiho," and the dogs start off. One of the half-wild Greenland dogs, who refused to be harnessed with the others, follows the sleigh at a swift gallop. The team and the three men grow smaller in the distance and vanish at last. But in the quiet ice-cold air we can still hear, for a long time, the clear call of "left" and "right" growing fainter and fainter.

15

A Trip to Reindeerland

It is a radiantly beautiful day. The sky is an Italian blue, the land and sea a dazzling white. With its scattered figures of ice, deep in snow, the fjord today resembles a parkland scene, hoarfrosted and dreaming in the sun. We stand on the roof of the hut and look around at the quiet world. There is not a breath of wind. The pure air is like fresh water from a spring.

Today all far-off things seem palpably close. Opposite us, with all its hills and hollows, Reindeerland gives the effect of a piece of sculpture that we can touch. The distance beckons us with wild strength. For the first time I feel the wanderlust that in spring seizes all those who winter here. I want to see at close range, to touch, to tread with my feet the tenderly gleaming country across the fjord, which seems so near.

"Shall we go across?" I ask Hermann. "Perhaps we'll get vitamins."

He is silent.

"Didn't you say that Sven Ohlson was going to be in his reindeer hut at the end of April, and didn't you talk about the possibility of our meeting him there? I would so like to get to know our neighbour."

"Hmm," is all the answer.

"I bet there's hundreds of reindeer grazing over there in the sun," I continue.

"Hmm."

"You think I won't be able to get across the fjord ice? That's a joke."

My husband sniffs the air, looks at the sky, and declares that today is not the right day for such a trip.

"But it can't possibly get any finer than this," I say, quite wild with impatience.

"That's it; it's too fine," says Hermann. "It's just the kind of day when someone who's inexperienced does the stupidest things."

"But what can happen?" I ask. "The weather will last for five or six hours. We'll find food in Sven's hut, and we can stay there a couple of days if the weather turns bad. I'll be responsible for this trip."

Hermann laughs, and lets himself be persuaded.

We leave everything in the hut as it is, strap on our skis, and put on our snow glasses. Apart from an empty rucksack and our guns, we take nothing with us. We start off straight across the fjord at right angles to the opposite shore. I would have liked to go further down the fjord, to see Nois' hut at the southern tip of the Reindeerland peninsula. I have heard that it is a crate turned into a dwelling, an aircraft crate that had been left at Kings Bay when Nobile started on his flight to the North Pole, and which Nois had later transported to Liefde Bay.

Nor do we make straight for the North Cape of Reindeerland, where Sven Ohlson's hut lies. For at that part of the coast there is said to be a strong current that makes the ice unsafe and begins to break it up in the early spring.

The further out we go, the higher become the ice masses piled on top of each other. The drift snow brought by the wind from every quarter has given them fantastic shapes. Some of them look like leafy trees, which cast deep, soft shadows. Now and again we come to places that are smooth like meadows under snow, peaceful in the sun.

"Those were the windless zones during the storm when the fjord froze over," Hermann explains, pointing to the broad, even surfaces.

"Windless zones?" I really have to make an effort to remember that this calm snowy landscape, which has been before my eyes now for months, and in which we are used to making our way so surely, is nothing but storm-tossed water whipped by frost and wind, and that beneath us the fish and seals are swimming, and mountains lie hundreds of yards below in the depths.

Every now and then I take off my snow glasses to enjoy the colours of the ice. The even surfaces and gentle slopes are a light carmine red, and everything that is turned away from the sun vibrates in the celestially pure colours of the spectrum, from lilac to the deepest and purest cobalt blue.

We have been on our way for about an hour when we catch sight of a gull, flying in a slow zigzag course low over the ice. "It's looking for bear tracks," Hermann calls out softly. And soon we come upon quite fresh tracks of huge paws. They run evenly from the sea down the fjord. We follow for a while and come to a spot where the bear has obviously halted. Two small white-furred seal flippers are lying on the ice, the remains of a meal.

"Of course, it's the end of April," Hermann says, "and the seals have already dropped their calves. They choose the inner fjords where the ice is firm. There'll be a lot of bears wandering down the fjord today." Calmly he stirs and probes, with his bamboo stick, the heaps of snow lying about, and sure enough he finds the little arch of snow under which the mother seal had bedded her young, thinking it well hidden from bears and foxes and the prying eyes of the large robber gulls.

"What will the poor mother seal say when it comes back and finds nothing but the chewed-up bones of its calf?"

"You shouldn't measure animals' feelings with a human scale," he answers soothingly, and goes on, looking for the best road between the ice floes.

Surreptitiously I glance back to see how far we have come from our hut. And I gape. Of the coast of Grey Hook nothing is to be seen. In its place rises a high perpendicular marble-blue wall that I have never seen before. Amazed, I call out to Hermann. All he says is: "High ground. Probably Wijde Bay, and perhaps a part of the north coast, reflected in the upper and warmer layers of air." I find it all terribly confusing.

We come across more and more bear tracks. The evenly spaced marks of their paws lead in winding lines between the hills of snow, all of them coming from the sea and going down the fjord. We are in the middle of the bear kingdom. All my fear of bears has vanished. As in a dream I go on through the splendid strange world.

How quiet it is here. The sun shines on a soundless scene. The magical hues of the soft shadows glow deeply. Everything belongs together here, even the bear tracks in the deep snow, which shows with what peace of mind the animals have gone on their way. Everything breathes the same serenity. It is as though a current of the most holy and perfect peace were streaming through all the landscape.

I feel that I am close to the essence of all nature. I can see its paths interlacing and still running alongside each other in accordance with eternal laws. I divine the ultimate salvation before which all human reasoning dissolves into nothing.

Is it possible for people in Europe to imagine the profound peace and the beauty of this gigantic wilderness of ice? When all the storms are ended and it lies in the sun? Can they know what they are doing when they tear a creature away from this vast harmony and drag it to the great cities? Do they know what they are doing when they cage a polar bear, this power-ful animal created to brave the most violent forces of nature, the lashing storms on the drift ice in the long winter night—a creature whose talent it is to roam over seas and frozen islands and icy lands, untiringly and restlessly through the immensities of the most undisturbed region of the earth?

The closer we approach the middle of the fjord, the larger are the fast-frozen icebergs. In the largest of them there are deep fissures and cracks through which the seawater has welled up and frozen fast onto the snow, transparent like pale green glass.

Hour after hour we go on through this stupendous and glorious world, which is constantly presenting us with new scenes. Reindeerland is growing clear and higher, the bear tracks more infrequent. We are held up by a wild confusion of ice boulders that it seems impossible to cross on skis, apart from the difficulties of the cracks under the snow. But at last we reach the coast. The rocky shore, in part overhung by enormous snowdrifts, in part sloping down to the fjord, has at its edge the same ribbed grooves and fissures as we have on our Grey Hook shore, deep curving cracks in the ice surface, running far back, made by the ceaseless rise and fall of the tides. The snow on the mainland is crisscrossed with the tracks of foxes. "Lots of foxes have escaped Sven's traps," we say simultaneously. All the tracks lead down to the sea. Creeping after the bears, the foxes at this time of the year find enough to eat in what the bears leave behind from their meals.

Reindeerland is not at all like what I had imagined it to be from the other side. There are no reindeer grazing in their hundreds; it hardly seems possible that this frozen land is the tundra, the reindeer's paradise. I feel tired and horribly thirsty. I can feel the icy wind, blowing direct from the north, that numbs my face. We are still far from Welcome Point, the northern tip of Reindeerland. The name was given to it centuries ago by Arctic seafarers, and it has remained a welcome point for the Arctic ships of today which, coming here from the east, where the danger of being crushed by the ice is greatest, find an open channel off the north coast of Reindeerland kept free by the powerful warm water currents from the west, usually as early as the spring. We have to reach the point today. Between it and us lies Sven Ohlson's hunting ground, and there he has his most easterly refuge hut.

For about two hours my husband leads the way, over hills and hollows that seem never-ending, over country from which it is impossible to get any view, so that I cannot understand how he will ever be able to find Sven's hut. But in the end we come out exactly at the right point on the coast, and there, far below us, looking quite tiny, is the small, snowed-up hut.

The frozen polar sea lies spread before us in all its immensity; in the extreme west and north there are a few narrow strips of open water, standing out blue-black in the vast whiteness. Its moving shimmer is fascinating, and we can hear, soft but still quite distinct, the surging of the tide. We stand a long time speechless, listening to the sound we have so long missed, and staring transfixed at that small patch of breathing, moving nature. And across in west Spitsbergen, above the white peaks of the mountains, clouds are gathering—real dark storm clouds. How long it is since we have seen a cloud! We are overcome by a sweet nostalgia. Nature is stirring, if only in the far distance, and to see it and hear it is for us an experience that can be gauged only by those who, like us, have lived for months in a world frozen to death. It is as though, at one touch, everything in us that is living springs up out of a long and paralysing sleep.

No smoke rises from the chimney of the little hut; we can see that well enough from a distance, in the clear air. So, Sven Ohlson is not there and it is a great disappointment. But since I am tired and hungry we make our way down. Around the little hut the snow is undisturbed, which means that Sven has not been here for a long time. The door of the hut, which opens outward, has been pushed inward; that can only have been done by a bear. As we can find no axe or spade or any other tool around the hut, we cannot get the door open. The cold—it is thirty-five degrees below today—creeps into our bones. At last I manage to squeeze through the narrow slit in the doorway and, from the inside, to twist the door outward.

At last we are in the cosy little hut where, on his last visit, Sven had made ready everything for our reception. There are knives and forks on the table, and a small dish of butter, with a note lying beside it: "Coffee ready on the stove. Bread outside in the passage." In front of the stove there is dry kindling, wood, and matches, and soon a crackling fire is burning. The coffee, to which milk and sugar have already been added, is thawing out and getting warm. We drink more cups than we can count, and it does us a world of good. And when we have thawed it out, we eat countless slices of the sweet-smelling treacle bread that Sven has baked of dark corn meal. Grateful for the thoughtfulness of the old hunter, we lie down for a while on the broad bunk by the side of the stove. The sun peeps in through the little window, which gives us a view over the broad Arctic sea. The little hut is sparklingly clean. It is said of Sven that he always carries on his sleigh a scrubbing brush, soap, and soda, and scrubs down every one of his huts before leaving it. The wooden walls are decorated with bright photographs. A number of girls' faces, pretty as pictures, look down on us. "Sven's got good taste," we both conclude.

"If you want to go out hunting from here," I say to Hermann, "I'll willingly stay here for a day or two alone in this charming hut."

"In which, if you fall asleep, you'll be a goner," he adds.

I find it hard to believe that one would die in a few hours in this friendly hut.

"Just think, stupid," he goes on. "There's neither an axe nor a saw here. How will you break up the enormous logs of driftwood outside? The small logs you've got in here won't last long. And then how will you cook and keep warm? And there aren't any sleeping bags either. The walls are thin, and if bad weather ties us to the hut we'll be out of food pretty quick. We can't count on Sven's coming here either; in weather like this he doesn't leave his hut at all."

Longingly I look out through the small window to Biscay Hook, to the little promontory jutting far out into the sea where Sven, "the most northerly Swede in the world", has for more than fifteen years lived alone with his two faithful dogs. There are two old Russian graves on the peninsula, with small crosses, and in the summer hundreds of eider ducks hatch their eggs there, around the hut. Sven's dogs are touching, Hermann says. When Sven has visitors and they talk together, the dogs, from their place under the bunk, wag their tails all the time and thump them on the floor because for years they have been used to their master's voice speaking alone, and only to them.

Crossing to Biscay Hook today is out of the question. It is more than thirty miles from where we are, and between here and there lie Rode Bay and many lagoons. Hermann is strongly in favour of returning home. He is conscious only of the bank of clouds coming up quickly from the west. We leave a note for Sven about our visit with greetings and many thanks for his hospitality, and we also leave the mail that Nois had left with us to forward to Sven when he visited us at Grey Hook.

We make the door fast and start back with heavy hearts because we have still found no game. It is night and frightfully cold. The sky is almost completely clouded. In the north the low red sun shines through tattered shrouds of mist. Its rays spread a livid light over the hills of Reindeerland, vanishing into the milky light of the snow. From the north comes the surging sounds of the sea in the open spaces among the ice.

We quicken our pace; we do not want to be caught on the ice by fog and snow, for we have not brought a compass with us.

It is about midnight when we again reach the fjord. It is grey, and covered with a damp and icy mist. We follow the tracks left by our skis when we came here, while the air begins to get thicker and thicker. The sun grows a deep copper red, and the peculiar atmosphere, which is met with only in the north and in the Arctic, envelops us, the indeterminateness of day and night, light and darkness, the extinction of all colours and outlines.

I have to call up all my energy to keep up the quick, even pace. My feet are aching with cold. My leather shoes were thawed out but not dried in the warmth of Sven's hut, and now they are frozen stone hard. The left shoe is constantly slipping out of the straps, and I have to bend down a hundred times to strap it in. Although I drank so much coffee, I am again tortured by thirst.

"Don't eat snow," Hermann calls out to me. "It makes you tired and still more thirsty. You'll have to control yourself."

The sky grows darker and a grey mist encloses us; the soft snowflakes begin to fall. If a wind should rise, obliterating our ski tracks, we shall be lost on the ice. My feet have grown quite numb, and for the first time I feel to the full the pitilessness of the Arctic world. Now I can understand the patience and the prudence of the hunters, their obedience to nature, their unconditional submission to its laws. Only in that way can they keep themselves alive, in their solitariness, through all the dangers of the land.

My husband goes ahead of me and does not speak. I know that if he were alone he would go more quickly, to avoid the fog and snow on the ice. We can no longer see the mainland.

The heavy damp air makes breathing difficult, and my limbs feel like lead. Judging from the bear tracks, we are about in the middle of the fjord. There do not seem to be any new tracks, and the old ones are almost obliterated by snow. Everything else is submerged in my weariness and apathy. I can scarcely keep my thirst under control.

Hermann amazes me. He does not feel thirsty; he steps out vigorously, turning round now and again to smile at me patiently. For him this trip is scarcely an exertion at all.

I do not know how many hours we have been on our way when the mists begin slowly to thin, and out of its dense veils rise the mountaintops of Bock Bay and Cape Roos to the south of the fjord, gloriously bright in the red rays of the morning sun. The whole chain of mountains becomes visible, glowing deep pink. The blue sky arches above them. We have reached the fair-weather zone of Grey Hook, the triumphant, clear ice atmosphere, further from the sea. The familiar Rillenberg Range comes nearer and grows larger. And on the flat foreland, a tiny black point, our beloved little hut. We seem to be still an eternity away from it when we make a surprising discovery.

Beside the ski tracks we made in the morning there are fresh bear tracks leading toward the hut. A bear returning from the end of the fjord seems to have taken an interest in our tracks. We can see how he has padded along beside them, and with his forepaws thoughtfully shuffled the snow to and fro across the tracks.

"It will be by our hut," Hermann cries out, his eyes sparkling, and involuntarily he accelerates his pace. I am too tired to be either glad or fearful; my only thought is that the bear may delay my going to bed.

But before long my husband slows regretfully down. The bear has not gone up toward Grey Hook, but has turned sharply away immediately below our hut.

Hermann races ahead to the hut. I can see smoke rising from the chimney. At last I am home, but the hut is ice cold. I take off my shoes. Both feet are dead and snow white. I sit on the bunk and howl with pain and swear. Hermann also swears, stoking the fire, grinding coffee, and massaging my feet all at once. He swears at women in the Arctic, their frivolity and obstinacy, which are quite out of place here considering how inexperienced they are.

The hut grows warm, my feet become alive, the coffee bubbles, and the leaven stirs and begins in its familiar way to give out its comforting smell. We sit down to breakfast and rejoice that we are at home. We have been away for twenty hours. And now we also know where the bears are, and Sven will get his mail. The sun is shining through the window. Grey Hook with its blue skies holds us again in its spell. Forgotten are the storm clouds and the open sea and all blissful thoughts of Europe.

But over the fjord and to the northwest the sky is darkened by mists. "There's a storm over there at Sven's place," Hermann says. "It's good that we went because weather like that can last for days."

16

The Fight for Vitamins

It is difficult to say anything about the state of mind of people who, according to medical standards, should have long been dead of scurvy, but who are still living quite gaily in a glorious world of glittering whiteness, full of sunshine, day and night. As dark as it was in winter, so is it now light, for a wonderful law of nature assigns to every spot on the earth a precisely equal span of time in the sun. To the furthest limit of our vision, land and sea are still frozen over. Temperatures are still between twenty and thirty degrees below zero, and there is no living creature to be seen. In all the brightness and beauty even the thought that we have now been eight months without any fresh meat can scarcely cast a gloom over our spirits; all our other food containing vitamins, such as butter and honey, have long been consumed, and the condensed milk is more than a year old.

Nor does Sven Ohlson seem to have had any luck with his hunting, for he does not turn up at our place. Pity! We would have been happy to have him visit us, even if he came without the gift of fresh meat.

Middle of May. Still no living thing to be seen except for one white gull, which one morning came flying by our hut under a white mist-bow. This phenomenon—the mist-bow, somewhat smaller than the rainbow of our latitudes, snow white and near—and the white gull brightly lit by the sun, were so beautiful that neither of us thought of our guns.

In any case Hermann has thought up a new theory. We do not need vitamins. The courage to face life and good humour are the best vitamins.

End of May. And today the first seal appears on the ice. I catch sight of him from the roof, early in the morning. At first we think it is the shadow of an ice floe, but looking through the field glasses we see that the dark spot on the pack ice is moving to and fro.

It makes us quite excited and happy. Immediately after breakfast we take our guns and start off after it. It is to be expected that the spot should vanish from our sight the moment we set foot on the ice. But my husband proceeds with the greatest confidence, zigzagging between the ice masses, and I follow trustfully. He gives me a lesson as we go along, telling me that when they are on the ice seals are very vigilant, keeping a sharp lookout all the time for bears, their greatest enemy. You have to creep up on the seal against the wind; they have a very acute sense of smell and very sharp hearing.

After an hour—for myself, I have long abandoned hope that we shall find our way to the spot—Hermann says that we will now have to creep forward on our bellies, and when the seal raised its head, which it does every twenty seconds or so, we must be absolutely still, without stirring, pretending that we ourselves are seals.

CHRISTIANE RITTER

So we creep on, our faces smothered in the snow and wringing wet from head to toe, but the guns have to be kept dry. I cannot help turning my head from time to time, so that any bear in the neighbourhood might not get the idea that we really are seals.

Soon the seal comes into sight. He is lying peacefully in the sun. Every twenty seconds precisely he raises his head and looks around him. We crawl further. For the first time in my life I feel the hunting fever. Has the seal got wind of us? Has he heard anything? Suddenly, without looking round, he hops to his blowhole, and plop, he has disappeared.

Greatly vexed, we return home, and as we climb the bank by our hut there is the seal again, lying peacefully in his old place.

The next day we try our luck again, for the seal is again on the same spot. We cannot follow the tracks left by our skis the day before because a light wind is blowing, and we have to make a wide detour to come up unobserved. We get to within shooting distance. The shot cracks out, and the seal disappears again into his blowhole. The bullet rebounded from a piece of ice, for the seal was lying in a fairly deep hollow.

The next morning he is not there. It is twenty-five degrees below and windy, and in these conditions no seal lies out on the ice.

Every day we go to look at the bear traps. Near Odden, on the sea ice, there is a black patch of water. Hoping to find birds there, we cross over. When we reach the spot we find that it had once indeed been a crack in the ice; but now the water is covered with a thick layer of transparent ice, and there is no trace of any living thing to be seen.

On the way back home we hear, from a dip in the snow, the gurgling of water and the chattering and jabbering of waterfowl, punctuated by a quite remarkable "A-hua". We can hear it all so clearly, as though we ourselves were standing by a lake surrounded by birds. But around us nothing is to be seen except frozen land and frozen sea; there are no patches of open water.

"It's an echo," says Hermann. The *waake*—patches of open water in the ice—may be far out to sea. The "A-hua" is the call of one the young male eider ducks, which come up here in the spring from more southerly parts to mate. There seem to be a good many birds there already, but we do not know because presumably all the patches of open water are far out to sea.

Reluctantly we leave the dip in the snow, where the chattering of the waterfowl has fooled us, meat-hungry as we are. A little later we spy, on the ice of the sea to the north, enormous black creatures. "They're bearded seals," says Hermann, "but we won't catch them. They usually lie on the broken ice close to a water hole."

Through our glasses we watch them, lying lazily in the sun and scarcely moving. But we are obsessed by the thought that somehow or other we could, with one shot out there, get over one thousand pounds of meat. At any rate we want to try our luck.

We start out on the ice at Odden and make for the animals. They take absolutely no notice of us; they seem to feel quite safe where they are. At a distance of about three hundred paces Hermann fires one shot. One of the bearded seals is hit, the others slip lazily into the water. Wildly enthusiastic, we rush toward it.

In front of us lies our mountain of meat. Then, suddenly, there is a dull jerk under our feet and around us, in a circle about ten yards from where we are standing, the snow gapes and sinks visibly. But the ice still bears, and we go on. Again the hollow sound circles us, but we are prepared to do our utmost. The seal is about a hundred yards away. Once more the beastly jerk, and the ice under our feet begins to wobble, it turns blue-grey in colour, and we sink up to our knees in ice slime.

Now we have to turn back and take off our skis. It is not at all easy to move forward on the slimy ice, whether with skis or without them. We are glad to get back onto firm ice and to climb up the bank. Inaccessible, the mountain of fresh meat is left behind. If we had a light boat we might risk the trip later on; but without it there is no chance of getting there.

The next day a *waake* opens where the bearded seals were lying, and a lot of birds are circling round. We have to be satisfied with the sight of them because we cannot reach the place. But with open water in the neighbourhood there is a better prospect that bears will come our way.

"Well, now that the current is beginning to break up the ice, there's no longer any chance of Sven coming over to visit us," says Hermann. Much later we learned that early in May Sven had shot a bear and that the faithful old hunter had started off with some meat for us. Unfortunately his dog sleigh overturned on the way and he lost his snow glasses in the snow. Completely snow blind, he had to break off his journey and let himself be led back by his dogs to Biscay Hook.

The weather changes. It grows bitterly cold and a storm breaks and lasts many days. We are chained to the hut. When the storm has passed, I have to shovel the door clear on my own. My husband has sprained his foot and is lying in the bunk.

So now, every day I go alone to inspect the spring traps. In addition to the rifle, which is supposed to give me a feeling of safety, I take with me my field glasses, with which I examine the traps from a distance. But they are so deep in snow that it is not until I get quite close that I can see whether there is a bear in them or not. I am always glad to get back from these trips, particularly when they take me along the coast where the ice floes, piled high on top of each other, shut off my view; many of them, while drifting ashore, have stirred up layers of sand and have exactly the same colour as bears.

For some days petrels have been flying along the coast, looking for places to lay their eggs. The first time Hermann comes out of doors again, he shoots a gull in flight.

We fall on the bird like hyenas; the two of us pluck it and we put it on to cook. Again and again we raise the lid and hungrily breathe in the smell of the meat, and before the bird has been cooked through we have already drunk the strong soup, which is dark green in colour from the oily fat.

The next day the gulls come in flocks, flying so low that Hermann gets sixteen of them in flight.

It is an irony of fate that the same evening the first bear is caught in one of the spring traps on Odden. Despite a fierce wind, Hermann goes out to inspect the traps and comes back with the joyful news. With knife and sleigh we make our way to Odden through the whirling snow.

The powerful beast is lying in front of the trap, a small hole in his forehead. It takes all our strength just to turn the bear over in order to skin it. It is freezing work in the storm. We have just loaded the pelt onto our hand sleigh when the gulls come, screeching and circling round the corpse.

Now we are rid of all our worries about food and begin to enjoy life. Our favourite trip is out to Odden, across which most of the gulls take their flight.

Here is the place with the glorious view, here, where on the spit of land jutting far out into the sea, Mathilas, the famous Arctic seafarer, has his last resting place; he did not want to leave his ship, in danger of being crushed by the ice, with its crew, and met his death in the sea before Grey Hook. A small black wooden cross sticks lonely out of the snow.

Grey petrels and ivory gulls fly above us, and above the gulls the returning auks. You are first made aware of them by their cry, and if you search a long time, you may perceive in the depths of the deep blue sky flying companies like small clouds of tiny bright stars. From those great heights they look out over the sea of ice for open spaces of water where they find their food. Flock after flock comes in from the south and flies north.

Around us the frozen sea, above us the deep sky full of returning birds. The consciousness of space and of unconquerable eternal life fills all our being.

17

Spring on the Ice

We are sitting on the black roof of our hut, which is now slowly beginning to emerge from the snow. More or less clothed, we are enjoying the warm sun and imagine that paradise has come to earth. Around us the Arctic spring exults in heroic splendour and purity, and in incomparable beauty.

Early in the morning we are awakened by the twittering song of the little snow bunting, the only singing bird on Spitsbergen. Of all places, he has chosen our chimney as his perch from which to sing. But when we creep out of our snow hole the little visitor has vanished. The high shimmering pink mists are still lying on the ice, and above in radiant white the high mist-bows thrown by the bright sun. As the mists clear, the boulders of pack ice rise like white phantoms, growing steadily clearer in their mirror-like hues, until at last the sea of ice lies clear before us in all its white immensity, dazzling in the sun.

Gulls in their snow-white plumage circle like eagles over the ice. With beautiful wide movements, slowly folding their wings, they alight on the glittering tips of jutting ice. Company after company comes flying past our coast. Here all form and all life is manifested in white against sunlit white.

We humans are surprising beings to be found here. All the gulls first circle once or twice inquisitively around us and our hut; sometimes they turn back from their onward flight and circle round us once more. The air is so still that we can hear the soft humming and whistling of their wings.

On the ice, seals are lying in their thousands. To the furthest distance the sea is sown with their black forms. They are enjoying the glorious sun after the long time of darkness, which they have to pass under the heavy blanket of ice. We no longer hunt in the neighbourhood of the hut. We are well provided with meat. A skinned seal is dangling from the ice axe on the roof, and its shadow travels round the hut, following the short deep shadow of the hut itself.

The animals are without fear, and around us they carry on their peaceful springtime pursuits. We can watch them quite close; to humans they seem touching, sometimes droll. A pair of mating Arctic terns have taken possession of the iceberg stranded on our shore. The iceberg is now no more than pointed, smooth, dripping ice. Around it the hollows are filled with pale-green seawater in which small red marine creatures are swimming. The terns are the most graceful and delicately etched aerial acrobats of the Arctic.

The female tern no longer troubles to find food for herself. She sits on the highest point of the iceberg and plays the coquette and gazes into the water. But the male tern tires himself out in the air. He hovers and flutters around in one spot in the air until he discovers in the emerald green pool a small sea animal, gleaming in the sun; then he drops like a plummet into the water, comes up and flutters over to the female, and while still in flight passes the morsel to her. She seems to be insatiable, wants to be fed three times a day.

And if another pair should want to share the nourishing pool, the iceberg owners start loudly scolding.

The outcry lasts until the newly arrived pair give up in resignation and fly on. In the evening whole columns of females sit around the larger pools in the ice, all of them turned toward the water, their long delicate swallowtails spread out behind them like trains. All the males are flitting and fluttering to and fro, dipping and diving and giving a gymnastic display. It is remarkable that we never saw any of the males feeding a female while this was going on; it all seemed to be rather a gala performance put on for their fair mates.

A particular beauty is our Klara, an Arctic ptarmigan who pays us several visits every day. So far she has turned up punctually every morning while we have been seated at breakfast. We heard the rushing beats of her wings through the open door, as she circled the hut, flying lower and lower and then settling slowly on the snow. There she sat near the door and waited. Of course she got her dainty morsel every day. A few days ago she began to bring her bridegroom with her, who is as beautiful as she is: snow-white plumage, black feet, and greenish-yellow beak. They come flying down, billing and cooing, a picture of perfect harmony. But there is an immediate change in the situation when Klara discovers something edible in front of the hut. She swoops down and pecks out huge hunks of the blubber. Her swain sits at a respectful distance. He may not advance a single hop, for then Klara cries "Gre-e-e," her neck stretched out and her eyes angry. Only when her gizzard dangles on one side and, gorged full, she is gasping fearfully for breath does the bridegroom dare to approach the blubber. Then he in his turn pecks greedily at the food and swallows uncannily large morsels. Then the two of them, their beaks open, gasp for air. Suddenly, as though by agreement, the two rise and fly off, light-winged into the air.

Even the *tyviu*, a satanic bird, is in a gentle and affectionate mood. Often enough, it is true, these black robber gulls with long tail feathers, screeching, pursue a solitary flying gull and try to rob it of the mouthful of food it is carrying, but for the greater part of the day the *tyviu* sits dreamily in the snow with his black and equally thievish bride.

Sometimes we creep out onto the ice when the *waake* are forming. There, sitting in the sun around the fissure of open seawater, which looks like a small lake in the snow, are the eider ducks. There is always a black female and one of the pretty black and white males, which come to the far north only in the spring. The birds are waiting for the land to appear before hatching their eggs. They are waiting in beauty and patience, a picture of utter peace.

The snow covering the ice of the fjord is full of the fresh marks of paws, for now the feast is spread for the bears. But in spite of the danger, the seals sleep peacefully in the sun. Often there are as many as ten or twenty of them, and only one of them keeping watch. The bear does not kill more than he can eat. Of a hundred seals fate hits only one. My husband has watched bears which, having eaten their fill, pad along among the sleeping seals looking neither to right nor left.

We often come across sleeping seals as we wander about. When they catch sight of us they start up and topple over each other in their hurry to be the first to get into their snow hole. There is one seal that has quite forgotten the bears, love, himself, and the rest of the world, and has become our faithful "house seal". Every day he rises, deep black, out of a small patch of water that opened a little while ago in front of our hut, and settles down on the ice. There he lies through many hours of the day and keeps us under constant watch. Only when we go away from the hut does he doze off lazily in the sun. Every morning he comes up, pleased as punch, out of the water and goes through the same manoeuvres. He slides onto the ice, glides along for a few yards, and then disappears again into the rift in the ice. Up he comes again, goes through some exultant acrobatics out of sheer joy of living, and, plop, he is under again. Ten minutes pass before he reappears once more, looks around, stretches himself luxuriously, and then settles down on the ice in a position from which he can best keep us under observation. In the sun, the colour of the seal steadily lightens. Now and again he changes his position slightly and continues to watch us. He listens with pleasure if we whistle a song to him. Everything interests him, but we must not raise our arms. That seems to remind him somehow or other of bears, and he at once disappears. Often he lies the whole night on the ice, staring inquisitively at the door of our hut.

The small rift in the ice turns into a large gap, running in a semicircle around our little promontory. Now and again we see the dark head of a seal swimming along, and since yesterday the love-struck eider ducks in the neighbourhood use it for their promenade swim. In single file they swim past, black female and black-white male. There seems to be a surplus of males, for we often see two of them exerting themselves about one female, and there are heartrending scenes of love rejected. But the dark ladies know what they are about. Far and wide there is no clear land nor any open water that is certain to remain open for the young ones which, as soon as they have been hatched, will be driven into the water. So the dark ladies go on sitting on the ice, and the white gentlemen sit by them. Now and again they give their call, "A-hua," almost dislocating their necks. "Huhu," the black females answer placidly, and go on staring into the water.

The only *waake* left within sight in the neighbourhood is the one in front of our hut. The animals come from near and far, to our extreme delight. Whole skeins of eider ducks come flying this way, and auks and small guillemots, which whip up and down in the water like little boats, turning with frantic speed on their own axis. A pair of proud black guillemots, looking like coal-dark swans with their long necks, make only brief visits to our *waake*. They dive and surface, smooth and black, and swim leisurely away. The seals swim around with obvious pleasure, making their way between the birds, which do not show any fear. There is at least one pair of every species in this *waake* of ours before Grey Hook, and we are irresistibly reminded of Noah's Ark. A profound law of nature distributes the species over the world. The sense of being at home seems to be equally strong in man and beast. Every living creature is drawn to the spot of earth on which it was born. The hunters have noticed that in spring the same birds return to the same places, even when, as sometimes happens, the conditions for breeding their young are very unfavourable. A gull with only one foot—the other had probably been shot off—is sighted year after year on Grey Hook.

Sometimes we climb the hills—not to keep watch on the ice nor to look for a ship. No, we are like all other inhabitants of Spitsbergen who fear the first ship that comes in the spring. Let nothing come to disturb our peace.

When we reach the spurs of the range we unfasten our skis and lie down on the moss that has now come through all over the southern slopes. Small poppies and crowfoot, which start to bloom under the snow, are growing among the moss. Right in front of us here is a bird cliff. Its stony rock falls so steep and sheer that no fox can climb it. In every single niche and hollow of the cliff a female bird is brooding over its eggs. Gulls have leased the ground floor, and above them the little auks have nested, and on the topmost rocky height sits the dominating figure of a burgo-master gull, proud and motionless, as though carved in porcelain. There is no peep, no cry of a gull to be heard. Gently, with cautiously beating wings, the male birds fly to and from the sea to feed the females. A deep peace, an almost palpable air of dedication, lies over the mountain. Full of solicitude and love, the parent birds await the new life that is in process of becoming.

A few snow-white gulls circle over us in the deep blue sky. The tips of their wings gleam in the sunlight. Everywhere the profound peace of the wilderness prevails.

Once, toward the end of June, we catch sight of the tip of a black mast between the broken ice floes to the north. Much as we have persuaded ourselves that we are indifferent to men and ships, the sight of the approaching mast fills us with blissful joy. A shot rings out, and our happiness is transformed into furious anger. They are shooting in our peaceful world! But then the ship slowly draws nearer, forcing itself forward along a narrow channel toward our coast. Someone is coming to visit us. We race out toward Odden. A boat edges into the ice and three men come striding across the ice of Odden. Without skis, they sink up to their knees in the ice slime.

The captain of the Norwegian Arctic vessel, Jens Ohlsen, one of those polar seafarers whose expeditions have made valuable contributions to our knowledge of the area, has come to call on us. He asks us how we are getting on, whether we need anything, whether he can be of any help to us in any way.

"No, we don't need anything. We've got everything we need. Nor do we want to leave here yet. The only thing is that our supply of coffee has given out."

We are entertained onboard ship, and are given a whole kilogram of coffee and four tins of condensed milk as well as a four-week-old newspaper. Then we return happily to our wilderness.

The *Vesteris* departs in all haste from our coast, for the narrow channel in the ice through which it had made its way to us is beginning to close. The next day it has entirely disappeared, and the ice lies thicker than ever.

But around the shores of Bangen Hook and Verlegen Hook the water is open, and on particularly clear days we can see, in the northeast, land lying like a white fairyland in the blueness.

We are seized by an uncontrollable longing for remote places. We want to go further and further into the Arctic lands, the islands in the ice, the frozen earth, which is still lying there as on the day that God created it. Europe, and everything that binds us to Europe, is forgotten. We have a wild longing, more urgent than ever before, and stronger than all reason and all memory.

The ice, which until now has been snow-white, begins to show blue and watery patches that grow larger and larger. Seals dive up and under where before the ice was unbroken. The fissure in the ice around our peninsula widens visibly with the wind until it is as broad as a river, and one day the whole gothic ice structure disappears slowly westward. In one single day, with the wind from the south, all the ice is driven out of the fjord. The floes race by our coast, fast as an express train. The sea breaks with a rushing sound on the ruins of the ice, and then the fjord is a sheet of blue glittering water. But further out to sea there is still ice.

All along the shore the black female eider ducks enter the water, surrounded by their young; and all the childless mothers, who failed to hatch their young in this particularly severe year, follow the ducklings as they swim past. Below, on the shore, something peeps up at us. It is our house seal, his neck outstretched, who has not gone off with the ice; he has stayed here and is still watching us.

We push our boat into the water and row across to the small high island to collect the deserted nests, which are made entirely of the most splendid down. We row for hours, without tiring, on the calm clear waters of the fjord where the depths of the heavens are reflected and single ice floes are carried slowly along by the tide. As they thaw, the water turns them into the strangest shapes. Some of them look like swans with widespread wings, others like the loveliest flowers. Others again still bear some of the snows of winter, tinged with lilac-pink shadows. Some of them, which have turned over in the water, gleam with glassy, emerald-green fungi. The ice fields are driven in again from the sea, but the land is free of all its snow—thawed out, crumbling, black Spitsbergen. Vast lakes of melted snow have formed on the foreland, and streams flow rushing past our hut down to the sea.

July passes and August comes. The male eider ducks have all flown off to the south, but our coast is still blocked by ice. The air grows cold and our shadows lengthen, and now and again thick mists cover the land.

Shall we have to stay here another winter? Without stores? Are we trapped, who in our blind love for the country have let slip every opportunity to leave it?

18

Spoilt for Europe

One day we hear the blast of a ship's siren out at sea. We recognise the *Lyngen*, sending us greetings. She has made her way through the ice.

We are overcome, half by pain and half by gladness; for now I must say farewell to Grey Hook and return home. Hermann is to come part of the way with me, to meet his comrades with the cutter at Sydgatt. There our ways part. In autumn, when the Arctic has been fished, and the winter stations have been stocked, the cutter is laid up at Sydgatt and each of the hunters makes his way back again to his solitary winter hut.

A motorboat makes its way between the ice floes to our coast. The captain has kept his word and has himself come to fetch us. He and his men help us to beach our boat and to make the hut fast against storms. Then we go back between the ice floes to the steamer. The engineer is pouring out bottled black beer to celebrate our return. A few seals accompany our boat, watching inquisitively.

Below, on the *Lyngen*'s small companionway, all the women are standing; they embrace me as though each of them were my own mother. A stewardess, her hair waved and a little cap on her head, laughs at the ragged passengers with faces burnt dark and clothes bleached white, their boots leached by seawater and stained with the blood of seals, who have boarded the ship.

A thousand questions and a thousand items of news rain down on us; we cannot take them in. The ship begins to move, the engines throb, and the ship's hull automatically drives off the ice floes on which the little auks and guillemots are sitting. Fearfully the little birds rise and let themselves drop into the troubled water of the ship's wake. A cloud of black smoke dances over the ice. Back on Grey Hook our hut grows smaller and smaller. The passengers stare at us, baffled by our love for the country that lies so black and bleak between mist and ice and water.

No, the Arctic does not yield its secret for the price of a ship's ticket. You must live through the long night, the storms, and the destruction of human pride. You must have gazed on the deadness of all things to grasp their livingness. In the return of light, in the magic of the ice, in the life-rhythm of the animals observed in the wilderness, in the natural laws of all being, revealed here in their completeness, lies the secret of the Arctic and the overpowering beauty of its lands.

Feeling slightly alien, we sit in the dining saloon among the passengers who are so smooth and polite and who are keeping up a lively conversation. The sauces and the savouries do not taste as good as they used to.

Facing us sits Björnes, the old winter inhabitant, in his dark blue fisherman's jersey. Yesterday, while on board, he shot a seal and cut it up in the hold. He is holding in his hand a hunk of seal meat from which he is sawing off pieces with his hunting knife. He pays no attention to the sauces and still less to the passengers. He does not look up, but he seems to feel that my husband and I are looking at him. He divines my pain at leaving the Arctic wilderness, and as though he still wishes to show me some kindness, he cuts off a large piece of the black, dry meat and holds it out to me across the table.

Christiane and Hermann Ritter

Christiane and Hermann outside the hut at Grey Hook in summer

The hut at Grey Hook, buried under the winter snow

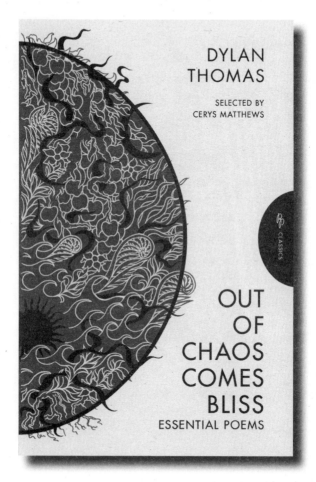

DYLAN
THOMAS

SELECTED BY
CERYS MATTHEWS

OUT
OF
CHAOS
COMES
BLISS
ESSENTIAL POEMS